An Introduction to the

# TELLINGTON-JONES EQUINE AWARENESS METHOD

## The T.E.A.M. Approach to Problem-Free Training

by
Linda Tellington-Jones
and
Ursula Bruns

With a Foreword by Ewald Isenbugel, V.M.D.

Breakthrough
PUBLICATIONS

For information address:

Breakthrough Publications, Inc.
Millwood, New York 10546

International Standard Book Number: 0-914327-18-6
Library of Congress Catalog Card Number: 87-72002

Manufactured in the United States of America
Second printing: June 1988
Third printing: May 1989

# Contents

# Foreword

The role of the horse in our modern world has changed dramatically. The versatile workhorse is now, for the most part, a creature of the past. Today's horse is primarily used for riding, a recreational companion to man.

The earlier methods of schooling and training riding horses were designed to produce a horse that was totally under control at all times — as well as one capable of hard work. Today's training goals are not much different. Whether used in competition, ridden for recreation, or, as is often the case, used for both, our horses must be safe, obedient, and ridable. The means to these ends, however, have changed considerably and are, as this book will show, being continually improved.

Better understanding of the behavior and psyche of the horse, more appropriate means of caring for his needs, and more subtle methods of training have not only improved the daily lives of many horses, but have greatly deepened the communication between horse and man, making their relationship richer. Indeed, many horse owners who care for their horses personally find in their daily contact with their horses as rewarding and joyful an experience as riding itself.

Despite all man's learned efforts, however, the horse remains an easily excitable animal, ever ready for flight. The pressures of our highly technological world and especially the great demands of equestrian sports often overwhelm him. At the same time, the days when man shared a common work day with his horse, from which an understanding of the horse's being and needs evolved quite naturally, have disappeared.

As a result, the horse suffers from stress, fear, and misunderstanding. Inappropriate reactions on the part of both horse and handler create a growing tension and uneasiness, which can even result in illness . This is where the Tellington-Jones method begins. Based on a profound knowledge of the psychological and physiological needs of the horse, Linda Tellington-Jones's method is, in fact, basically an age-old, holistic method of handling and training the horse. She works first on the mind of the horse, using signals easy for the horse to understand—gestures, postures, and the voice. This trust-developing communication is then supported through a system of analytical touch, using contact with the hands in varying intensities on different regions and points of the horse's body with quieting, softening, relaxing, and possibly healing effects. Not only is a basis for trusting communication developed, but the horse's own physiological energies are activated to improve problems of the most disparate physiological and psychological natures.

Finally, building on this foundation, the actual work of training can

begin, using in-hand exercises developed by Linda herself. These exercises make unusual demands on the horse's ability to learn as well as on
his muscles. They aim at activating his unused mental and physical
abilities.

This integrated program results in a more relaxed, calm horse — a
pleasant, safe mount. A closer, more trusting relationship develops between horse and rider. The horse's self-confidence grows and his overall
performance improves.

Linda Tellington-Jones has demonstrated the value of these simple
and ultimately sensible approaches for years now before the eyes of fas-
cinated audiences all over the world—from the biannual "Equitana" con-
vention in West Germany to the Hippological Olympic Training Center
in Moscow. Now, with Ursula Bruns at her Equine Test Center in Reken,
West Germany, Linda has developed the training program described in
this book. This is a method that can be learned and practiced by anyone
who wants to work with horses.

For their pioneering work in this area, I would like to thank both of
them, for myself and in the name of all horses.

Ewald Isenbugel, V.M.D.
Professor of Equine Breeding
School of Veterinary Medicine
University of Zurich

# Acknowledgments

I wish to thank Maria Brosche, "Bruggie" Bruggemann, Margaret and Bernt Schmidt, and Christina Schwarz for the tireless hours they spent keeping records and working with the twenty horses who were involved in the five-week test program which was the basis for this book.

My special acknowledgement and thanks to Roger Russell, who traveled and taught and worked with me during the first eight years of the formation of T.E.A.M. His background in the field of science played a major role in our exploration of ground exercises which would enhance the learning ability of horses. And I am forever grateful for his genius and tireless energy in building new courses for testing "nonhabitual" movements. It was Roger who coined the phrase that describes T.E.A.M. philosophy so well: "It's easier to influence a few pounds of brain than 1000 pounds of muscle."

My deepest thanks to Annagret Ast for coordinating the training of T.E.A.M. teachers in Europe, and for publishing a German version of the T.E.A.M. Club newsletter.

I wish also to thank Cornelia Guest and Sheryl Studley for their wonderful support in editing this book from the German translation. And my heartfelt thanks to all the dedicated horsepeople around the planet who have participated in clinics or have read about T.E.A.M. in magazine articles, and to those who have taken the time to write to us and share their experiences.

Without my sister Robyn Hood, who teaches T.E.A.M. clinics on three continents and has participated with me in the unfolding of the work from the beginning, T.E.A.M. would never have spread as it has. My eternal thanks for the astounding energy and enthusiasm with which she publishes *T.E.A.M. News International* and responds to the mountainous stacks of mail.

For all of the horses and humans whose lives have been effected by T.E.A.M., I wish to thank my coauthor, Ursula Bruns. Without her insistence and encouragement I would never have thought of organizing T.E.A.M. into a method, and without her this book would not exist. During the five-week test project Ursula took over 3000 photographs and spent countless hours discussing the process. Subsequently, T.E.A.M. has been taught at her Reken Test Center to thousands of grateful horse enthusiasts.

Linda Tellington-Jones

# Introduction

Welcome to the world of T.E.A.M.

T.E.A.M. is an acronym for "Tellington-Jones Equine Awareness Movement," a revolutionary approach to working with problem horses.

T.E.A.M. also stands for the partnership which, with the use of this method, can evolve between you and your horse.

Beyond that, T.E.A.M. represents the tens of thousands of horse-owners around the world spreading this new awareness and understanding between horse and human.

The T.E.A.M. concept was organized into a teachable form in 1978 at the encouragement of Ursula Bruns at the Reken Center in West Germany.

T.E.A.M. is now practiced in twenty-two countries on six continents, including the United States, Canada, Iceland, England, Belgium, the Netherlands, Norway, Sweden, Finland, West Germany, East Germany, Poland, Austria, Switzerland, France, Sardinia, the U.S.S.R., Australia, New Zealand, Argentina, and Brazil. There are now T.E.A.M. centers in Australia, Canada, Germany, Austria, Switzerland, and the U.S.S.R., as well as at four locations in the U.S.—Colorado, New Mexico, Maine, and Texas—where both horses and owners can come to learn.

I had been searching for solutions to problem horses since 1944, beginning with my first horse who bucked me off on a regular basis. The solution of my seven-year-old mind was to clip clothespins to my mare's ears. Throughout my junior years in Canada I trained and showed horses in hunter, jumper, English and Western pleasure, and equitation classes, specializing in "catch-riding." By the age of sixteen I was training and teaching professionally.

In 1961 my husband, Wentworth Tellington, and I started the Pacific Coast Equestrian Research Farm at Badger, California, for the clinical study of the training and management of the horse. One of the programs at PCERF was a residential school for riding instructors and trainers, which combined daily extensive academic study with four hours of riding instruction. The program was based on the use of psychology in place of force for the training of both horse and rider. Participants were required to compete successfully in combined training, dressage, English and Western pleasure, and endurance riding. Over the course of its thirteen years, this school, the first of its kind in the U.S., attracted students from nine countries and thirty-six states.

It was here in 1971 that I first met Ursula Bruns, the editor and publisher of the German magazine, *Freizeit Im Sattlel*, an alternative magazine for the recreational rider. In subsequent years, we were to spend countless hours discussing riding and training techniques. From these discussions came dozens of articles which lead to Ursula's creation of a unique eleven-day course for the beginning adult rider, known as the Bruns/Bahr Method, emphasizing fun, relaxation, and stress-free learning. Thousands of adult riders from all over Europe have graduated from this revolutionary course.

From 1975 to 1978 I began teaching weekend and ten-day clinics to adult riders with problem horses at locations all over Europe.

During the summers of these years I completed professional training the the late Dr. Moshe Feldenkrais at the Humanistic Psychology Institute in San Francisco. Dr. Feldenkrais, an Israeli physicist, was known for his breakthroughs in handling physical dysfunction in humans and for maximizing athletic performance. He believed that the human nervous system was capable of learning through a single experience, without repetition, with the use of nonhabitual movements, as long as they were nonthreatening and did not cause pain.

I began to adapt this idea to work with problem horses. The concept that we could change a horse's behavior in a few lessons was totally revolutionary. I had believed, like most horsepeople, that a horse could learn only through repetition. During those four years of working with hundreds of adults with their problem horses, I developed a series of ground exercises. With minimal use, these exercises resulted in permanent personality and behavioral changes. It was at this stage that Ursula Bruns urged me to formalize my work into a teaching system. We agreed to hold a five-week clinic at Ursula's facility in Reken, which she would photograph and record. Twenty horses from all over Germany were sent by owners, trainers, and veterinarians—horses for which their owners held no hope. This book is the result of that experience.

Twelve of the horses spent three weeks with us and eight only two weeks. The ground exercises were designed to simulate typical environmental stresses. Each day all the horses had an opportunity to gain confidence and overcome fear by successfully negotiating obstacles. In the beginning they were worked in hand and later under saddle. Four of the horses did not respond fully to the ground exercises alone because discomfort in their bodies prevented them from learning. The simple methods of the Tellington Touch provided the additional tools necessary to reach these horses.

On graduation day, these previously uncontrollable horses stood quietly and worked softly without halter or any other form of restraint.

The materials in this book were originally designed for the amateur rider. Since then, T.E.A.M. has been used by amateur and professional alike. However, the assistants who helped test these methods at Reken were single-horse owners who had never trained a problem horse before.

Please keep in mind you do not have to use all of these exercises all of the time. T.E.A.M. is not the only answer. You can combine T.E.A.M. with any method of training you are currently using. T.E.A.M. is for all horses, regardless of breed or discipline, whether you are a pleasure rider or an Olympic contender. You will find that you and your horse will benefit from any portion of this work. Even minutes a day will bring great rewards.

Trust yourself, and let your horse be your guide.

Linda Tellington-Jones
San Francisco, California
August, 1987

An Introduction to the

# TELLINGTON-JONES EQUINE AWARENESS METHOD

# CHAPTER ONE

# Communicating with the Horse

Before we begin any discussion of actual training methods, we need to focus first on answering two basic questions. First, how close is our relationship with our horse—how well do we know him? Second, what do we actually want to accomplish?

In answer to the first, many of us don't have a close relationship to our horses at all. We see our horses sporadically—at feed times, on the weekends, perhaps for an hour in the evenings, or for the occasional hack.

Imagine now an earlier age. Imagine the lives of shepherds, nomads, coachmen, farmers, and soldiers spent in close contact with their horse—sharing with the horse the strain of hard work and the joys of an hour's rest. How dependent upon each other they were; how close, in a way we can hardly imagine. In comparison, man and horse are often estranged in today's world. This is especially true when the horse is living not with us, but kept instead at a local stable.

Fortunately, interest in the being and psyche of the horse has never been as great as it is today. Intelligent riders are now aware that carrots and treats are not the key to communication. They are reading widely and studying the growing collection of excellent literature devoted to the psychology of the horse.

How, though, can we turn all this theory into practice? How will we be able to actually get closer to our horses in our daily communication with them?

This is where the answer to the second question becomes important. *What do we actually want to accomplish?* How close do we really want to get to our horse? To what degree do we want to allow him the play of his own personality, his own will, his own feelings? Is he supposed to think? Do we want to develop self-reliance in our horses? Do we want intelligent participation?

Are we even willing to grant that the horse *has* intelligence? Perhaps not creative intelligence such as man possesses, but nevertheless an intelligence basically capable of learning, and not merely of learning through repetition, but capable of drawing independent conclusions from learning experiences? We, the authors, do believe the horse is capable of this kind of learning. Our work, our relationship with the horse, and this book are all based on that premise. In this book where we've used words such as "think," "ponder," "follow mentally," and "consider," we've meant them in this nonanthropomorphic way.

Our goal is to train a horse to participate intelligently. Having both spent more than half a lifetime teaching riding, we have become committed to this goal for the following reasons:

Such a horse is

- *safer*, because he does not run away or shy in unfamiliar situations;
- *safer*, because he has learned to listen to his rider and to seek solutions together with the rider;
- *more of a pleasure*, because he gives his rider the feeling of really being one of a pair, of having a partnership on which he can rely;
- *less stressful*, because the horse does not have to spend his emotional energy fighting the commands of the rider and can instead focus this energy towards the pleasure of both;
- *a better performer*, because he can understand what we want of him and is more willing and able to learn.

The method outlined in this book is based on the assumption that no one really has more time or opportunity for the training of the individual horse than his owner. All of the exercises have been designed so that they can be done in immediate sequence or spaced at greater intervals.

These exercises can be done with any horse. You can even start a foal with the first exercises. In those years in which your horse is too young to ride or drive, he can still learn lessons that will help him later become a perfect riding horse. He can be trained to move in a balanced way; his interest in new things can be awakened; and his trust in man can be strengthened. The exercises are also effective with green horses in their initial schooling and with problem horses that we want to retrain.

In glancing through this book the first time, don't be put off by the minute detail in which you'll find some exercises described—exactly how to move your hand, how to bend your body to the right or left, how your horse is to execute a single step. None of this is superfluous. This method derives both its meaning and its success from such attention to detail. This is a method distilled from years of practical work, observations, and considerable teaching experience. It is based on a thorough study of the latest knowledge regarding the theory of movement in both man and horse as well as on studies regarding the ability of both to learn. It reflects in all its detail the opinions of leading scientists in these disciplines throughout the world.

These careful steps enable your horse to be more receptive to learning, as their detail does not overtax his comprehension. His successful learning experiences make him increasingly confident in his abilities. His interest in these multifaceted mini-exercises grows. He soon learns to pay attention to your every move, to every tone of your voice, to every gesture of the whip—and to connect with these an action he is capable of performing. He derives pleasure from understanding you as quickly as possible and from embarking on ever-new learning adventures with you. Of course, he will also be getting to know you, his teacher, thoroughly. If you take the time to go through the steps slowly and thoughtfully, your horse will grow to trust you explicitly because he will understand what you want of him.

You will also get to know your horse thoroughly. Soon you will be able to sense immediately when he is afraid, when he hasn't understood, when he is being overzealous, and when you need to repeat an exercise. As you begin to see the success each day brings, you will learn to control any impatience you might understandably feel. Soon you will be able to make your signals more subtle, and your horse will seem to participate more and more willingly. If you were once afraid of your horse, you will have lost that fear.

Although this book doesn't specifically deal with actual riding, Ursula would like to relate an experience she had in Ireland, years ago, with a horse that had been trained perfectly to think for herself: "I had been invited by acquaintances of friends to go hunting and was given to ride for the occasion a very valuable Connemara-Thoroughbred mare, even though her owners had never seen me ride. I felt a bit ill at ease and worried out loud that I might unwittingly do something to ruin the horse. The owner replied in an unconcerned tone, 'I've been told that you've ridden a lot. Just grab the mane, go with her, and don't do anything else. The mare has been trained to be totally self-reliant.' I did as I was told, and this ride became one of the core experiences of my riding life. It was a fast hunt chasing rabbits through a countryside full of jumps. My horse looked for her own spot in front of every jump, never stumbled, and jumped securely. Her own thorough enjoyment of the experience was tangible.

"In my fifty years in the saddle, on travels that have taken me throughout the world, I have always enjoyed most those horses that have been trained to think for themselves."

Following years of work and experimentation, we finally arrived at a simple scheme for the structure of this book—one which will first of all allow you to experience as fully as possible the process of the discoveries as we did at Reken and then help you to glean maximum profit from the resulting ideas for your own work.

We'll first introduce you to a particularly difficult horse, describing him to you as his owner did to us in our questionnaire and, later, as we found him. We'll then present the techniques that were used to gain the very specific insight into the horse's character and conformation that was necessary in our investigation. We'll then outline the procedures that were chosen, first to diagnose, then to correct his problems.

We also used specific tools in our school to teach the horses. These were the dressage whip, driving reins, a variety of obstacles, the touch of the human hand, a sensitivity to the horses' reactions, and a learning program that does not overtax the horse's comprehension. We will be describing these tools and their use in detail in individual chapters. We'll then demonstrate how they were used to attack the various problems that were encountered. As each of the horses brought along a different set of problems, the methods varied. Finally, all these elements, like small stones in a mosaic, will form a complete picture of a program appropriate not merely for the problem horse, but for every horse.

Let's now get to know Kaishan, who will illustrate for us the scheme described above.

# CHAPTER TWO

# Kaishan:
# A Case History

Kaishan is an eight-year-old purebred Arabian. He was castrated very late and still exhibits strong stallion mannerisms. He belongs to a lady who rides him two to three times a week for an hour and a half. She is becoming increasingly afraid of his behavior under saddle. Kaishan is excitable, canters in place, screams, and hurls himself sideways to block other horses in the group. He throws his head up and to the left, causing the underside of his neck to bulge out and making him hard to hold back (figure 1). Should he glimpse another horse off in the distance, he makes a blind dash in that direction, thoroughly terrorizing his rider.

His former owner had galloped him for the first six miles of every ride to keep him manageable—an impossiblity where his current owner lives.

Kaishan also behaves badly when not under saddle. He fights being tied and groomed, doesn't stand still, screams continuously, yanks himself free from the lead, and tries to attack any horse that comes within his reach.

## OBSERVATIONS

Kaishan was very studdish. He would find himself a mare and defend her so aggressively that we had to separate the two from the other horses in the field. He would bite other horses and repeatedly attacked them during turnout. He'd even try to bite at rivals while he was being ridden.

**Fig. 1**

He had no interest in people whatsoever. While being worked in hand in the outdoor ring, for example, he would notice a mare grazing at a distance and would try wildly to get at her through the enclosure, stretching his neck forward and screaming like a stallion. He paid absolutely no attention to the individual working with him at the time.

Under saddle, Kaishan would become completely distracted by the presence of other horses and throw himself sideways to block their way. He was excited and nervous. As a mount, he was no gentleman and considered himself the boss.

## INITIAL INVESTIGATION

We examined Kaishan from three perspectives:

1. We studied his head and expression for clues to his character (see page 16–18).

2. We explored his body with our hands, looking for possible sore or tense areas (see page 30).
3. We took a close look at his conformation and stance, trying to detect possible irregularities of conformation that could be at the bottom of his problems.

## ANALYSIS

1. Kaishan's head (figures 2a and 2b) shows him to be a reasonable individual of average intelligence who should have no difficulty learning. His ears are of normal length, crescent shaped, and delicate, set wider at the tips than at the base—a sign of stability of character.

The slight convex bulge of the nose—from where the halter sits to the nostrils—is called a "moose nose." This nose combined with the dish face—a sign of timidity—indicates a complex character and could account for his "bully" attitude. Aggression comes from a base of fear.

Kaishan's forehead is flat, displaying a single whirl in the hair pattern, which indicates an uncomplicated individual. His eyes are set wide apart and positioned well on the sides of his head, a sign of intelligence.

His front profile is slightly dished and is quite flat in the area between his eyes.

Kaishan's nostrils are large and delicate, a sign of intelligence. His

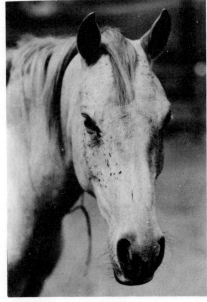

**Fig. 2a**          **Fig. 2b**

somewhat long mouth and set chin are signs that he can be difficult at times.

Both the form and angle of his eyes are unusual. Kaishan has the habit of never looking at the person working with him— he steadfastly refuses to look at the person. It's as if he doesn't want to see anybody close to him. He is completely disinterested in what's being done with him and gives the impression that he's retreated totally into himself. There is an indication of light-sensitivity.

Perhaps the eyes are the key to his problems. When a horse doesn't see well, he feels insecure. This robs him of trust. Furthermore, an insecure horse often throws his head up, ever ready to flee. When a horse habitually carries his head up, the muscles of the lower neck soon become overdeveloped. Then, as the underside of the neck gets pushed forward, the horse will drop his back, causing, in turn, constant pain and tension. This unhappy horse then becomes a "problem." This effect is also common in the horse that throws its head up for reasons other than poor sight.

2. Our second investigation uncovers important clues to why so many problems can accompany what appears to be such a normal individual with average intelligence.

Exploring his body with our hands in search of possible areas of pain, we are surprised that Kaishan reacts immediately to slight pressure applied just behind his withers by dropping his back and having a spasm under the contact. This would explain his strong forward impulsion, his "hot temperament." All horses will run instinctively from pain. If light pressure can cause Kaishan to cringe and drop his back in pain, how great must be his pain under the weight of saddle and rider? Each time he drops his back to our touch, he throws his head up automatically— just as he does under saddle to escape the rider's hand. Under saddle this habit has made him practically uncontrollable (figure 1).

Kaishan also shows definite signs of being in pain when we press behind his ears or on both sides of his neck at about the fifth vertebra and along the crest of his mane. We now know what the root of his problem is. If we take another look at the photo showing him under saddle, we can clearly see that his behavior has created a vicious cycle. The weight of the rider is uncomfortable to him, which causes him to rush forward, which prompts his rider to hold him back. He throws his head up to elude the hand of the rider and in doing so cramps the muscles of his neck; in her attempt to get him under control and slow him down his rider then turns his head to the left, making the painful cramping of his neck even worse.

A third strong focus of pain, we find, is at the point where Kaishan's

Fig. 3

Fig. 4

neck connects to his chest. This pain, too, is caused by his inner tension, caused in turn by carrying his head in an uncomfortable position. Such pain can also stem from being strongly pushed with the seat and legs into an ungiving hand. Arabians in particular can't tolerate this. Even the lightest pressure on this spot causes Kaishan to throw his head up (figure 3).

3. Finally we look at Kaishan's body from all angles (figure 4). Examining his conformation soon reveals another reason for his painful back. His back is very low, much lower than that of the average horse. It is also quite dropped and concave. For this reason it would be best to ride this particular horse in a Western saddle. His shoulder is also very straight. His legs and pasterns are good and his upper arm is long and strong. He has short, well-positioned cannons, and good, healthy feet and heels.

Sometimes a horse will have a painful back because his heels are too low. Thin, weak pasterns or pasterns that are too long are further possible reasons for pain in this area, as is a back that is too long or a shoulder angle that doesn't match the angle of the pasterns. Kaishan's problems, however, don't originate in his basically healthy legs but in his low back, steep shoulder, and high head carriage, which triggers the flight reflex.

The strong tendency for Kaishan's lower neck muscles to protrude, which gets worse under saddle, also contributes to his painful back, as does his inability to move freely and in balance, which results both from his conformation and from his having been ridden incorrectly. His first owner sat full and heavy in the saddle, driving him into the bit, a way of riding that can have catastrophic consequences for a sensitive Arabian, especially one with Kaishan's conformation problems.

## RESCHOOLING

This process is actually what this book is all about. Following our analysis of Kaishan's head and conformation, we began to reschool him with the T.E.A.M. program. We intend to familiarize you so totally with this method that you will be able to use it successfully and derive from it the greatest possible benefit.

After we've described all the necessary elements of the program thoroughly, we'll return to Kaishan and use his case and the examples of five other problem horses to demonstrate the use and effectiveness of the T.E.A.M. program in daily training. Although we've used problem horses for our case studies, we want to emphasize that any horse can profit from this training program. A happy, relaxed horse will also appreciate the attention paid to him by his owner and from day to day will participate with growing interest and will improve his athletic ability. A disinterested horse will become more alert; an interested horse even more involved. All horses improve with T.E.A.M. work, psychologically because they understand much better what we want from them, and physically because they learn to move with more coordination and balance.

It is our common conviction that a happy horse makes for a happy rider. We'd like our readers to keep in mind that the work we're about to describe is, in the end, something that not only benefits the horses, but benefits we riders as well.

# CHAPTER THREE

# Personality: The Clues

Looking at certain details of horses' heads to determine their inherent character is not a new idea. Experienced horsemen have been making judgments about character for centuries. Horses with extremely small, sunken eyes were said to be difficult. Horses with Roman noses were thought to be bold or stubborn. Big round eyes were generally thought to be a sign of friendliness.

Linda tells: "I grew up with a grandfather who was a well-known jockey and racehorse trainer, known for his ability to 'talk' with horses and understand their characters. As long as I can remember I have been interested in the differences in personality and 'intelligence'—or learning ability—of horses. In 1975, I had the opportunity to study a 'personology' course. This is a study of the shape and measurements of the human head to determine personality and inherent talent. This course stimulated me to refine the study of horses' heads to a degree that I could present the information to persons who did not have the opportunity to observe the hundreds of horses necessary to make these judgments—in such a way that the average horse owner can 'see' horses in a new way: as individuals with varying degrees of intelligence and ability to learn."

This ability to determine character is useful when determining how to train a horse. Is he basically a slow or fast learner? If he is slow, lessons may have to be repeated often and very made clear. If he is a fast learner he will be easily bored by repetition that is generally said to be necessary to train a horse. A smart horse who is bored often looks for ways to amuse himself—not always to the advantage of the trainer. If a horse is basically stubborn he is not the ideal horse for a beginner or a timid rider. A timid or sensitive horse would be unsuitable for a man who wants a tough, hard-knocking horse for hunting or polo. An intelligent rider would find it boring to work with a dull, slow-learning horse.

## STUDYING THE HORSE'S HEAD

One evaluates a horse's character by looking at the ears, the eyes, the forehead, the profile, the nose bone, the nostrils, the mouth, the lips, the chin, and the definition of the face.

### Ears
Are the ears long or short? Fine or wide at the base? Close together? Each shows a different character. Lop-eared horses such as the old-type Hungarians and Trakehners are known for their dependability. Long, stiff ears set close together at the top and the base indicate a tendency to be changeable and unreliable. Horses with extremely short ears are generally difficult. The ear length is naturally relative and must be judged against what is normal for the size and breed of horse.

### Eyes
The eyes are probably the most changeable part of the head. Is the look in the eye hard, soft, proud, staring, dull, sad, frightened, introverted, friendly, trusting, wary? The look in the eye can be changed completely by working with a horse. (A horse that is dull and disinterested can become trusting and happy from the work in hand when it is interesting, stimulating, and fun for him.) The shape of the eye will also vary greatly. Are the eyes round, oval, triangular, extremely wide-open, immovable, half-closed? If the horse shows white in his eyes frequently (unless he is an Appaloosa who has the "human" eye or a large blaze) he is said by many horsemen to be crazy. Horses with this tendency usually have body pains that are unknown to the rider.

The round eye is generally found on a friendly horse. The half-closed eye usually indicates lack of intelligence. An eye that is triangular with several folds directly over the eye indicates that the horse is unsure—similar to a questioning frown or worried look. A deep depression above the eye indicates a hard life or severe sickness.

It makes a difference if the horse's forehead is wide between the eyes or narrow. A wide and flat forehead indicates a horse that learns quickly. Narrowness between the eyes shows he is not so smart. This, however, is not always undesirable. A school horse or a horse for a beginner is often better when he is not too smart. The horse that learns quickly can also learn undesirable lesson quickly. Once a narrow-faced horse has learned a lesson he usually retains it and can be an excellent worker.

### Profile

A horse's profile is very important. A straight face indicates an uncomplicated nature. A dished face shows timidity, and a Roman nose indicates boldness. A Roman-nosed horse with a "pig" eye (small and set deep in the head) will usually be inflexible and difficult, but a Roman-nosed horse with large, round eyes set well apart could make an excellent horse for hard work. The Argentine polo ponies have this type of head.

Bulges between the eyes indicate a difficult character, and a slight bulge just below the eyes indicates a quirk. A "moose nose," a bulge on the lower part of the nose, belongs to a strong character. Herd leaders usually have such a bulge.

### Mouth and Nostrils

A squarish muzzle usually indicates an uncomplicated character and a muzzle that slopes sharply from above the nostril to the upper lip indicates a complex character, usually with many ideas—particularily if the upper lip is loose and active. Typical of this characteristic is a horse Linda knew in Germany who amused himself one day by picking up a sheep by the back and walking around with him. When his owner yelled at him he dropped the sheep and turned around with a look as if to say "Who, me?" The loose, active upper lip generally belongs to a horse who is curious about everything and likes to make contact with things.

It is amazing how many variations there are to the nostrils. They can be long or short, immobile or very movable, with thin or thick edges. Generally the larger and more movable they are the more intelligent the horse is. A narrow, underdeveloped nostril can be a sign of nearsightedness. When such a nostril is combined with a dull, disinterested eye and ears that don't prick forward but rather stay mostly to the sides with little movement this often indicates a really mentally deficient horse. Wrinkles over the nostrils are often a sign of pain (when accompanied by accelerated respiraton) or of disgust, an expression that one sees often on older horses with much character.

The length of the mouth is also an indicator of character—the medium length being desirable, the short mouth usually belonging to an inflexible and stubborn horse, and the long mouth indicating a very sensitive horse. A horse with a puffy or full area at the top of the mouth generally has stubborn streaks. One should be careful not to get in a fight with such a horse as he will often become more stubborn.

### Swirls

The swirls or whorls on the face also tell much about a horse. The Arabs, gypsies, and Philippinos had theories about character related to the swirls. Even today in the Middle East the Bedouins put much worth on the body swirls when deciding the price of a horse. Linda was first made aware of the swirls by her American grandfather who rode race-horses in Russia before World War I, and who had a gypsy interpreter who taught him about the meaning of swirls on the head. At the Pacific Coast Equestrian Research Farm in California (of which she was co-director), Linda did a study of 1500 horses in 1965 to determine character related to swirls.

The variation of facial swirls and what they determine about character includes the following:

*A single swirl between or above the eyes.* This is seen in the majority of horses. The reports on personality of such horses were in the range of normal, generally uncomplicated behavior. With such a swirl, discount its use in evaluating personality and look only at the facial structure.

*Two swirls adjoining* (either one above the other, above or below the eyes, or beside one another). This combination has proved to be the most significant over the years. This indicates a tendency for an unexpected or uncalled-for emotional reaction. Such a horse could get "silly" or upset without reason. If handled quietly he will settle, but if punished or handled roughly he could get hysterical.

That doesn't mean a horse with two adjoining swirls isn't a good horse. This information is only a general guide and it holds true only about 70 percent of the time. With the T.E.A.M. technique most of the idiosyncrisies we just accept as a part of a horse's behavior can be changed.

*One long swirl* (either above or below the eyes). These horses enjoy more than average contact with humans. Horses with this swirl that are not friendly have usually been abused or are in pain.

*A swirl located several inches below the eyes.* A high percentage of such horses were reported to have the desire to "amuse" themselves— often at the owner's expense. Such habits as turning on water faucets, opening stall doors to excape and often freeing other horses, and untying the most complicated knots were reported. Some horses with this behavior do not have low swirls, but the majority of horses with these swirls had such inclinations.

## ANALYSIS

This character analysis may seem all very complex and it is. It is always a question of *combining all the features to determine the final outcome*, and that takes experience. It is worth the study, however, as the information can be very useful.

For example, Linda recalls a horse she was asked to look at in Canada in May of 1981: "He was a Quarter horse who was nice to handle on the ground but had run away with his young owner several times, and she had been advised to sell him. He had an attractive head with large, round eyes, set well apart, and his face was flat between the eyes. His ears were of medium length and wider at the top than the base. His profile was straight. His nostrils were not large and not small, just average. His mouth was an average length and the chin was not tense. He generally had a friendly eye. His head indicated to me that he must have some problems in his body that bothered him. Sure enough, when I checked out the girth area and sides with my hands he laid his ears flat, telling me with his only possible means of communication that he was afraid of contact in that area. When questioned, the trainer admitted that the horse had been spurred and generally abused before the young girl had bought him two months before. I showed her some exercises to do with him to get rid of the fear and tenseness of having a leg near his sides, and now his rider—through understanding the problem—knows what to do to help her horse.

"If the same horse had had a small, sunken eye and a Roman nose or a bulge between the eyes or a stone-hard chin or other indications of a headstrong, willful, or sour character, my advice would not have been to keep him."

One should always clearly understand that with work on the body and T.E.A.M. ground exercises many of the inherent qualities of character can be changed. A horse that is a slow learner can become smarter with T.E.A.M. exercises. Horses who are inflexible or stubborn can become cooperative and a real pleasure to own.

Just by becoming aware that such character analysis is possible horse owners have the chance to see their horse in a new way—as an individual—and that knowledge can bring the interested horseperson much additional pleasure.

## PHOTOGRAPHIC EXAMPLES

We'll use the following photographs as models for observation.

**Figure 5.** This horse has a most interesting head. Both the descending angle at the end of his nose and his long upper lip point to a horse capable of many "amusing inspirations." His long mouth signals sensitivity; his soft chin, intelligence. This is somewhat contradicated by his poorly developed jowl and the narrow shape of his eyes. With such a contradictory combination, much about this gelding will be determined by his training. He could develop in many directions and is capable of a quick change in attitude. A good trainer could do a lot with this horse.

**Figure 6.** This is a rather difficult mare. Her eyes, set low on her head, show intelligence. Her ears are of good length and aren't too close together. However, her extremely short mouth and tightly drawn chin point to a stubbornness that makes this a complicated personality. The mare's owner was a beginner and lacked the experience to understand her and treat her properly. This is not a beginner's horse!

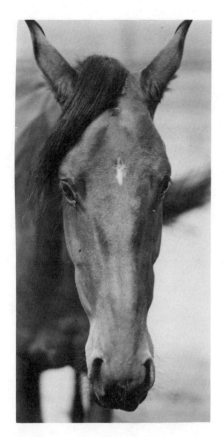

**Figure 7.** We see here a long, narrow face. This mare's medium-sized eyes are set fairly high on her head, a sign that she won't be a very quick learner. Her nostrils are rather narrow and point to a lack of curiosity. Her ears are long and positioned well apart. She'll be reliable once she's understood a concept. One will need a lot of time and patience with her, however, as she won't pick up on new ideas as quickly as many others. Once she's learned a lesson, though, she'll retain it and perform dependably. This characteristic is often more desirable than the ability to learn quickly. Horses who are quick to learn are just as quick to learn undesirable habits. The bond between man and this horse must be developed and continually fostered with patience. Only through patience will she be able to develop fully as an individual.

**Figure 8.** This horse was the slowest learner in the program. The lack of definition of his head is the clue to his mental unclarity. His slanting eyes were half-closed much of the time. He was asleep mentally. His jowl is small and the plane of his face has no differentiated characteristics. However, his nostrils are medium-sized and have good definition, indicating an ability to learn. With T.E.A.M. work this gelding woke up and in one week was learning as fast as the others.

**Figure 9.** The bony protrudence or "quirk bump" on the bridge of this horse's nose under the eyes warns of unpredictable behavior. He was often very friendly and cooperative—and just as often, plain sour. He had once bitten his owner badly on the cheek and, on another occasion, chased a vet out of the pasture. When the trainer put his foot down energetically, however, this horse would co-operate. However, he was quick to become bored. This horse was not suitable for a beginner.

**Figure 10.** This horse's long, fine nose with extremely large, delicately outlined nostrils; her firm lower lip; her long mouth; and her clearly defined upper lip all point to unusual intelligence and sensitivity. This mare was wonderful to work with, as long as she was approached with understanding. Before she came to us, she'd been badly treated and had simply become impossible. She'd been described to us by her owner as independent and headstrong; however, she was immediately co-operative when the lessons became interesting and when we treated her with respect.

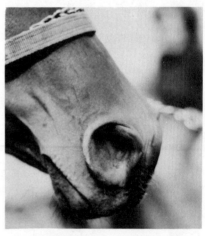

# CHAPTER FOUR

# The Tellington Touch: Work on the Horse's Body

## GETTING TO KNOW YOUR HORSE'S BODY

Just as every horse owner should get to know his horse's personality, studying the horse's head and all its individual characteristics for clues to his personality, so should he get to know his horse's body.

Many behavioral problems such as biting, kicking, nervousness, bucking, head-tossing, or rearing are generated by pain or tension in the neck, back, hips, or other areas of the horse's body. This premise is one of the fundamental principles of T.E.A.M. work. Discovering and correcting these problem areas with the Touch, combined with the ground work, is the T.E.A.M. key to reeducating your horse.

The objective of probing and exploring the horse carefully with the flat of your hand and fingertips is to detect areas in the horse that are tense or sore, or areas that are warmer or cooler to the touch than the rest of his body. This kind of inventory of the horse's body enables you to understand him better. Perhaps you'll discover areas of sensitivity, discomfort, or pain of which you had no previous knowledge. In working on the areas of your horse's body you'll be using pressure of varying degrees with your fingertips (see page 28). Some horses will react to light pressure by throwing up their heads, twitching muscles, or even jumping to the side. Others will not respond except to the deepest of probing.

If a horse drops his quarters while being mounted, or drops his back in response to being merely groomed or saddled; if he persists in a disunited canter or tries to take off when asked to canter; if he knuckles behind; or if the muscles of the withers and back twitch constantly, the problem is almost always caused by pain. Even beginners can be successful in pinpointing the origin of this kind of pain by systematically probing the horse's body.

Work in a secure and quiet area so your horse won't be distracted. You're going to explore his body with your hands. Throughout the process you must use your eyes, your other senses, and your ability to empathize with the horse to be always alert to his every reaction.

You may not feel successful in your first session. Don't give up. The sensitivity of your hands and your ability to perceive your horse's slightest reaction to their touch will develop. Also, developing a reliable sense of which reactions are normal and which might indicate pain requires practice. No exact knowledge of anatomy or the muscular structure of the horse is necessary to get to know your horse's body in this way. It will simply take time to develop an intuitive understanding of your horse, letting him tell you, in effect, about himself.

## GROOMING

Your work on the horse's body will go beyond the beneficial effect of discovering areas of pain. It will make you aware of how potent a tool you have in your hands for creating well-being in your horse. Having taken the horse from nature to use for our pleasure, how good it is to know that we are capable of giving him pleasure in return. Watch how horses in a herd stand close, "massaging" one another along the neck, withers, back, and croup with their teeth. We can emulate some of this pleasurable act with our hands.

A well-mannered horse should stand quietly while being groomed and should allow himself to be touched anywhere—on the eyes, ears, nostrils, lips, mouth, chest, shoulders, withers, back, loins, girth area, belly, udder or sheath, along the hind legs, and under the dock of the tail. Most horses, however, have spots they don't like us to touch. They clearly demonstrate their nervousness or displeasure by contracting muscles, stepping to the side or rear, or even kicking out. We often ignore or misunderstand the real meaning of these signs. *A horse has only this body language of movements and reactions to tell us that something is wrong.*

An otherwise friendly horse who dances nervously around when being groomed or who tries to bite is trying to tell us something. Perhaps we've hit a hidden wound or a painful swelling in the saddle area. Or perhaps he's simply saying that we're being too rough. Horses who don't want their backs curried or brushed, who duck away from any touch in this area, and who may even begin to tremble in anticipation of being touched here, are trying to tell us that their whole back hurts. Many horses cannot stand being touched on the belly or on the insides of their legs. They are probably ticklish or very sensitive, and their reactions are purely reflex action.

Few horses like being touched about the head any more than we would like a stranger feeling around on our faces. Many horses especially dislike being touched around the nose, lips, and eyes. For us to enjoy being touched in these private areas of the face, we must like and trust the person doing the touching. It is the same with horses. Only when a horse trusts and likes us will he enjoy the touch of our hands. However, once he has begun to enjoy being stroked, we will have established a new and very special route of communication with him. We will also have prepared the horse for having his teeth floated or for having the vet tube him, give him a shot, look into his mouth, or worm him. The horse will know that we will proceed in an understanding and careful manner.

## ROOTS OF THE TELLINGTON TOUCH

How do we win over our horses to this extent? How can we help once we've discovered that he is in pain? Indeed, is the lay person capable of this at all?

The common way of solving problems with horses is through simple disciplinary methods—either from the saddle or from the ground. We tried new linaments, new saddles, and different bits, and sometimes, in fact, we made surprising progress. But often this progress was too dependent on the ability and knowledge of a single trainer. Because these successes were so intimately tied to the experience of a single horseperson, such methods could not be methodically imitated by others.

From her studies with Dr. Feldenkrais, Linda brought a wealth of new insight and intensity to our years of common reflection on theoretical and practical work with horses.

According to this world-famous scientist, nonhabitual movements of the joints activate new neural pathways to the brain, activating new brain cells. Very simply, it is possible to activate considerably more brain cells if the body is manipulated in new ways, outside the patterns with which the brain is familiar, or if nonhabitual movements are carried out.

These insights that have been clinically proven valid for human beings have also proven true for horses. In this chapter we will describe new, unfamiliar ways of touching the horse. When and wherever we touch the horse in an unaccustomed way, new brain cells are activated and new reactions released.

Let's explore just one of the many possible examples. Time and again we come across horses who for years have refused to let their ears be touched. Sometimes the problem is so severe that the headstall must

be unbuckled to bridle the horse. Most owners of such horses have somehow learned to work around this problem. Often vets have been unable
to find anything wrong with the horse's ears, even after the most careful
examination. When we begin to work with such horses using the Tellington Touch method based on Feldenkrais's work, we discover over and
over again that these horses are also very sensitive to being touched at
the poll and on the neck directly behind the ears. Our experience has
shown that such a horse will allow us to touch his ears after about half an
hour if we begin farther back on his neck, sometimes even on his back,
and knead our way back up the neck to the poll with our fingers. Often
the horse will then let us being to softly "massage" the area behind the
ears, even to take the ears and pull them upwards softly to move them
around in gentle circles. The problem more often than not lies not in the
ears themselves but in the poll, specifically where the ligaments of the
neck connect with the head.

Linda reports of one incident: "I became quite sure of this while
working with a well-schooled dressage horse in Toronto who would not
let his ears be touched. He would shake his head and try to pull away
even when touched lightly on the poll. His reactions were equally strong
if touched on the crest or withers. Further attempts made it clear to me
that his ear problem, in fact, extended from the skull along the crest,
over the withers, and into the back. Once this had been established, I
began to work this area carefully. After about thirty minutes the horse
seemed to understand that I had grasped the connection and I was able
to touch his neck, poll, and ears without difficulty. Nor did the owner experience further difficulty after I had shown him how to proceed."

Based on Linda's many experiences and years of effort, the Tellington Touch came into being. This is a system of touching the horse's
body, head, and skin that is based on the teachings of Dr. Feldenkrais in
human medicine. From this technique of touching the horse's body with
the hand, a multifaceted system has evolved that actually has very little
in common with better-known techniques of skin and muscle massage.

The basic difference between our method and more traditional
methods is determined by the methods' ultimate purposes. The goal of the
more traditional massage is to stimulate the circulation and relax the
muscles. This can be very helpful in many cases but requires rather exact
anatomical knowledge. If a tense muscle is massaged too vigorously or incorrectly, the body feels threatened and the area feels more painful following the massage than before. In contrast, the basic goal of the Tellington
Touch is through the softest manipulation, incapable of generating any
harmful side effects, to activate new brain cells and release new nerve impulses. This improves the health, performance, and security of the horse

and the general sense of well-being of both horse and handler as it heightens the understanding between them. For this reason it is especially important that these exercises be done by the rider or owner himself.

To these body manipulations based on the Feldenkrais system, we added some easy-to-learn acupressure points as well as *Chua K'a*, a skin-rolling technique used for centuries in Mongolia. We feel that any horse, regardless of age or training, will benefit from the resulting system, the Tellington Touch.

## HAND POSITIONS

There are four basic techniques for working with your hands on the horse's body:

1. Using the hand held flat to relieve tensions, calm anxieties, and increase circulation.
2. Cupping the hands, holding the fingertips softly together, then pressing carefully with the fingertips to move the skin and muscles in small circles of about ¼ to 1 inch in diameter. The degree of pressure you use depends on the overall sensitivity of your horse as well as whether you are looking for pain and tension, using the Touch to relieve pain and inflammation, or stimulating new nerve impulses in order to give the horse an expanded awareness in a particular area of his body, for example, to lengthen his stride or increase his overall performance.
3. Slapping the horse over his entire body with your hand held lightly cupped. This technique is very useful before a horse show to stimulate the blood circulation following one of the other techniques described above. Usually you'll begin with the more heavily muscled parts of his body, such as the croup or upper arm. Cup more softly along his ribs, shoulders, and neck, and softer still on the back and loins. Be very sensitive to your horse's reactions to these cuppings and regulate the pressure of your touch accordingly. Cupping is used to desensitize a very nervous horse who can not stand still for even the lightest touch. This method is also used to wake up a horse before competition after a relaxing session of the Touch.
4. *Chau K'a* or skin rolling. Take up the skin between the thumbs and fingers of both hands and roll it in straight lines. We usually begin by moving these rolls of skin in long lines from the girth area back towards the flank, remaining parallel to the horse's back. Move the rolls across the shoulder, up and down the neck,

and finally up the front and back legs.

Skin rolling is an age-old technique used by the Mongols. It activates the circulation and helps to break up habitual patterns of tension.

While you're practicing these techniques of touch, be aware of your own breathing and the position of your body. Both animals and people tend to hold their breath when concentrating. This is counterproductive. If you'll breathe deeply several times, you'll find that your horse's breathing will also improve. Your sensitivity and feel will be compromised if you tense yourself by holding your breath. Try standing quite supplely with your weight balanced between the balls of your feet and your heels without locking your knees.

With practice, you'll become increasingly aware of the individual parts of your own body as you work on your horse. This increased body-awareness contributes clearly to increased self-awareness and general good health.

## PRESSURE OF THE TOUCH

To clarify the amount of pressure that can and should be used, we'll establish a conceptual scale from one to ten.

To imagine the first degree of the scale, put your second and middle fingers as lightly as possible on your eyelid—just enough to have control. Now move the skin of the lid in circles five or six times. Actually move the skin, don't just slide the fingers around on the surface. To get a more accurate sense of the feel, support your thumb on your cheek and allow the inside of your arm to lie loosely next to your body. Having felt this lightest degree of the scale, try to recreate this feel as you touch your upper arm—where you have enough muscle to feel a difference in pressure—with the same amount of pressure.

Next, press against your eyelid as hard as you can without causing actual pain. Now use this same degree of pressure against your arm. This is the third or fourth degree of touch.

Finally, press into your arm (not your eyelid!) with three times this pressure and move the skin in circles. This will be degree nine or ten.

With practice, you will readily be able to determine the gradations.

## SOME GENERAL TIPS

Before we begin with our actual work, here are some general tips. As we've said before, many horses don't like being touched on the head. For this reason it's best to start on a horse's body in an area where he likes to be touched. Be sensitive to your horse's reactions to the different touch techniques. If you're getting through to him, he will soon begin to chew, lick his lips, breathe deeply, and lower his head and neck. It will take a while for full trust to be established. It may take several sessions for your horse to accept the Touch.

If your horse moves away from your touch, use a lighter touch and move to a different spot on his body. A tense horse or one in pain will pull away from touch in a sensitive area. If you were to persist in touching him there too soon, he would become mistrustful. Your horse will tell you where he's sore or tense by throwing up his head, swishing his tail, stepping away, or threatening to bite or kick. Gradually approach and work the sensitive areas. Dressage horses often have particularly painful areas in the poll. Jumpers often have pain in the shoulders and between their forelegs.

As you work your way around both sides of your horse's body, he will get used to the touch of your hand and begin to accept it. At the same time, you will develop a greater sensitivity to your horse's reactions and of how strong the relative pressure can be that you can use.

## SUMMARY

The Tellington Touch is a completely new method of influencing the horse. Specifically it can be used
- to teach the horse to control his natural instinct for flight, and to substitute this with trust;
- to locate and relax tensions throughout the body;
- to establish a special, nonverbal means of communication between man and horse;
- to give the horse a greater sense of self-confidence and self-control.

Then, when coupled with the ground exercises which we'll describe in the ensuing chapters, the method
- increases the horse's ability to learn;
- prevents overreaction due to stress, even in competition horses;
- helps to lengthen his stride and coordinate his movements and balance (even highly schooled horses can profit from this);
- helps to prepare the young horse for the pressure of saddle and tack and the rider's weight;
- and finally, though of primary importance, as it strengthens the trust between horse and man and as such is the basis for everything else, the method gives us a means of actually contributing to the well-being of the horse.

## THE TOUCH IN PICTURES

In the following pictures Linda will lead you through the Tellington Touch.

### *The Back*

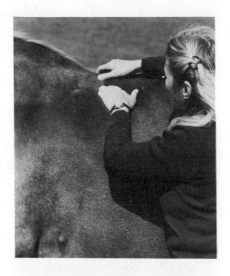

**Figure 11.**   To explore for tension or soreness in your horse's back, press into the area behind the withers with your fingertips. If your horse has a spasm, moves aways, swishes his tail, or throws his head up he's telling you he's sore or sensitive in that area.

**Figure 12.**   To relieve soreness or tension in a horse's back begin by placing your hands flat on the back several inches apart. Push the skin slowly upward. Hold a few seconds and then slowly return the skin to where you started.

**Figure 13.** Take your position facing the horse's back. Your horse's back may be sensitive or tense no matter what kind of work he does.

**Figure 14.** Place your hands over his spine behind the withers and press your fingertips into the skin with soft, push-and-pull motions. If the horse is free of pain, his back won't change position, but you can see that this horse's back has dropped several inches in comparison with the first picture.

**Figure 15.** This area of the croup is commonly sensitive to deep prob-ing with the fingers. If your horse is uncomfortable with the pressure, work several inches away and gradually work in toward the sore area using less pressure.

## The Neck

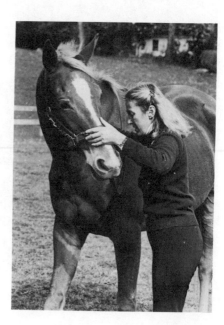

**Figure 16.** Bending the horse's neck in both directions improves his confidence, coordination, and balance. Starting with one hand on his nose and the other on his neck right behind his ears, slowly turn his head around toward your body.

**Figure 17.** Repeat the movement on the other side. One side is usually stiffer than the other; your horse will raise his head if he feels discomfort. As soon as you feel resistance, bend him in the easier direction again. Then return to the stiffer side and turn his head only as far as he wants to go. Be careful not to push his neck or to force him in any way.

**Figure 18.** As his confidence increases and he begins to relax, he becomes more supple.

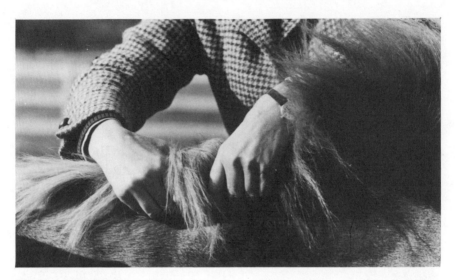

**Figure 19.** Next, move to the crest, starting close to the ears. Place your hands across the crest so that your fingertips are on one side of the neck and the heels of your hands are on the other.

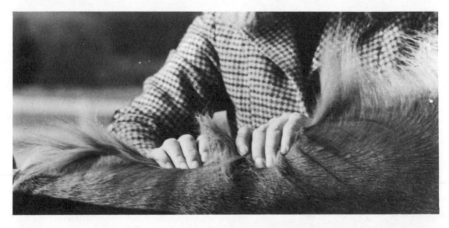

**Figure 20.** Push down on the fingertips and roll the crest away from you with the heels of your hands. Work up and down the neck like this until the horse's slow breathing and contented expression tell you he's relaxed.

**Figure 21.** If the horse is sensitive about being touched behind the ears, place one hand flat on his forehead and the other just behind the ears and below the crest. Hold your fingertips together lightly, press them softly into the neck, and move them in circles. This movement rarely fails to convince the horse to drop his head and accept your hand on his crest.

For the horse that's deathly afraid of having his mane pulled, you should add another step. Run your fingers through the mane, pulling gently downward to train his nervous system to accept pressure on the roots of the hair.

**Figure 22.** Move to the sides of the neck and build on the relaxation you've created. First place one hand gently against the windpipe to restrain the horse while your other hand explores his neck with a soft, rhythmic pressure from your fingertips; then work on both sides at once. Push in and slightly downward against the skin as far as your arms can reach. Finish with a vigorous shaking to relieve the neck of any lingering stiffness. Cup one hand over the crest and the other over the windpipe and shake the neck from side to side.

## Skin Rolling

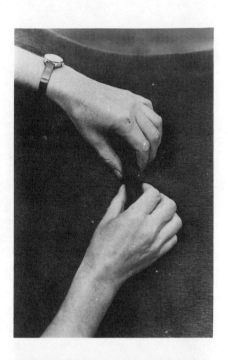

**Figure 23.**  Skin rolling is an easy exercise that the horse enjoys over most of his body. You start by gently picking up a fold of skin on the horse's barrel between your thumbs and fingertips.

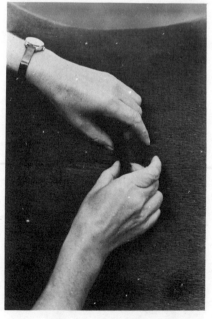

**Figure 24.**  Move the skin held between the thumb and fingers forward by walking your index and middle fingers forward. This movement can be done all over the horse's barrel, neck, hindquarters, and legs—wherever you find some loose skin.

**Figure 25.** In certain spots, such as the chest, you can actually pick up a bunch of muscle and roll it back and forth.

## The Face

**Figure 26.** Work on the face next. Start with the things you know he enjoys most. Place your hands flat against either side of his face with your thumbs touching his nostrils. Then move the skin in fast, gentle movements, bringing the left hand down as the right goes up and vice versa.

**Figure 27.** Then place one hand flat against his upper lip and move it quickly but gently, first around in a circle and then up and down.

**Figure 28.** Steady his head with one hand on the halter and insert the other hand over his top gum, just under his lip. Rub back and forth, and then run your thumb all around the inside of the bottom lip.

**Figure 29.** Finish by cupping your hand around the bottom gum and rubbing gently back and forth.

**Figure 30.** Next place one hand on his forehead just above the eyes and use your other hand to do the circular motion with your fingertips that I described earlier (see figure 21). This movement reinforces his confidence before you move on to the ears. He drops his head; he's listening; you're working as a team.

**Figure 31.** Put one hand flat on the horse's face. Cup the other hand around the base of his ear and pull gently toward the tip. (If you find that the ears are caked with fungus inside, be careful. The fungus makes the ear sensitive.)

**Figure 32.** When your horse is completely relaxed, remove his halter and continue. I like to remove this last barrier as soon as the horse is concentrating; being worked on without being restrained at the same time gives him a new feeling of cooperation.

**Figure 33.** Then pull the ears down and waggle each ear in a slow circular movement. Horses learn to love this. You can tell how effective this is by the way the horse drops his head, closes his eyes, and sighs.

**Figure 34.** The horse loves skin rolling on his face too. Cup one arm under his jaw to steady his head and use the other hand to roll the skin as you did on his body. Walk your fingers up his face, across his nose, and over his cheeks.

**Figure 35.** Next, steady his head and explore his face and eyelids with your fingertips, using a gentle but firm pressure.

## The Tail

**Figure 36.** Push the tail up and away from your body and rotate it first in one direction, then in the other.

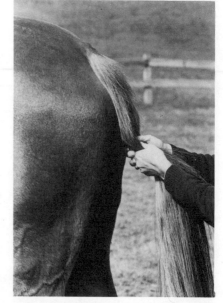

**Figure 37.** Next, flex each vertebra all the way to the end of the tail by rotating your wrists forward and back to bend the tail gently, first away from your body, then toward it.

**Figure 38.** Grasp the tail about twelve inches from the root with both hands and rock gently backward. Hold the pressure for about four to five seconds and then *very* slowly release.

**Figure 39.** A rhythmical "cupping" with the hand on the croup, hindquarters, and shoulders is used to wake your horse up after you've relaxed him all over with the Touch. Cup lightly on the barrel, back, and neck and more firmly on the large, muscled areas of the shoulders and croup. This cupping brings new feeling to insensitive or unresponsive horses. It is essential to cup your horse if you've used the Touch to relax him before competitions or strenuous exercise.

## The Legs

The leg exercises do not have to be done at the same time as the body work.

Fig. 40

Fig. 41

**Figure 40.** Start by picking up the leg by the knee and bringing it forward. With your hands cupped just behind the knee, swing the lower leg gently forward and backward, checking to see if your horse is relaxed or tense by the degree of looseness. Then circle the knee in both directions several times.

**Figure 41.** When your horse is comfortable with the knee circle, extend the leg, keeping the knee slightly bent. Hold the leg with one hand on the hoof and the other under the fetlock joint and circle three or four times in each direction.

**Figure 42.** Flex the leg at the knee and pull it back a little way.

**Figure 43.** I finish with each front leg by placing it down gently with just the toe touching the ground. This position teaches the horse to maintain his balance and keep his shoulders relaxed.

**Figure 44.** Next, circle each hind leg in both directions around the spot where the horse normally stands. Then pull each leg out behind him to encourage him to stretch. Guide the leg back, keeping it low. Do not force it. It's important to hold the leg relatively low. If you pull the leg up and back too far you could cause him pain in the lower part of his back.

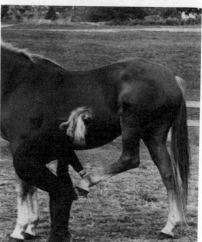

**Figure 45.** Then pull the leg forward under the belly and circle it in both directions.

**Figure 46.** Finish by placing his toe on the ground. These exercises help the horse to relax, lengthen his stride, and improve his balance.

The horse is relaxed. He has given you his full attention and you have helped him gain a new perception of self by working the various areas of his body, making him more fully aware of its individual parts.

# CHAPTER FIVE

# The T.E.A.M. Method: Ground Exercises

## OVERALL GOALS
## OF THE T.E.A.M. GROUND EXERCISES

The team ground exercises accomplish the following:
- the horse's confidence increases as he develops a greater awareness of his body. (This is also the case with people. See page 28);
- his coordination and movements improve;
- his sense of balance improves;
- he obeys without constraint, and develops self-control and patience;
- he becomes a keen observer, paying exact attention to detail;
- the basis for mutual respect and rapport between man and horse is established.

All this is grounded in our perception that horses are far more intelligent and have a much greater capacity to learn than is generally acknowledged. And, secondly, that when associated neither with fear nor fatigue, learning progresses much faster than was previously thought possible.

## GENERAL REMARKS

To get the most out of your T.E.A.M. work keep the following general thoughts in mind:

1. It is not necessary to do all the exercises each time you work

your horse. The art of leading will require more practice than all the more complicated-appearing ground exercises and for this reason should be reviewed on a regular basis.

Successfully negotiating three or four obstacles a day will make a visible difference in your horse. He'll be more patient and obedient, and his interest will grow perceptibly. Every exercise has a different effect and stimulates different nonhabitual body movements, each stimulating various neural pathways. These exercises need not be repeated on a regular basis; it will suffice if you review them from time to time. You will be surprised how quickly previously learned material will be recalled and performed flawlessly.

2.   All T.E.A.M. exercises can later be done under saddle. They should, however, be started in hand so that all tensions and anxieties that a horse under saddle could react to, or which the horse has already associated with being ridden, don't impede the learning process. Often when a horse approaches a new obstacle under saddle, he assumes his habitual tense posture. In contrast, the ground exercises are designed to teach a horse to move in new ways to release tension. His coordination and balance improve, which also improves his work under saddle.

3.   Contrary to popular opinion, horses enjoy company while being schooled. Not only does the company of other horses not seem to distract them, but it tends to stimulate better performance. Having several teams working together at the same time increases the enjoyment of all and creates a more pleasant working environment. Sometimes several teams will be working over the same obstacle: one horse is led through while the others stand around and watch. At other times, different teams will work on different exercises. The horses learn to be more patient, and horses who are afraid of or aggressive toward other horses learn to overcome these problems.

The program's goals for the horse are to teach him to
- stand quietly while tied, either alone or with other horses without acting aggressively towards them;
- stand quietly while being examined, treated, or groomed on any part of his body;
- lose all fear of the whip and accept movement of a four-foot-long whip over his entire body;
- walk, stop, and trot in a straight line, halting on command;
- walk and trot in a straight line three to six feet to the right or left of the handler, with the whip controlling the distance;

- "walk" and "whoa" while being worked between two hands with the whip and chain lead;
- longe on a short line at the walk and trot;
- work in the labyrinth whereby the horse learns
  - to respond to subtle movements,
  - to wait for signals (or spoken commands),
  - to accept the whip;
- back in a straight line and through an L-shaped maze to teach him balance and to prepare him for work under saddle and for backing from a trailer;
- walk and trot through cavelletti or crossed poles set at various distances either next to the handler or following him at a distance of from three to six feet;
- work through the star pattern;
- work through the grid;
- work through barrels;
- lead over, between, and under plastic sheets;
- ground drive with reins attached to the halter;
- lead over the "seesaw" and "bridge";
- lead through tires;
- work through all obstacles without a·halter;
- stand like a statue for grooming or while waiting for the next command of the handler;
- perform all exercises both from right and the left.

### Training Aids

For our basic training program you'll need
- a sturdily built, correctly fitted halter with large buckles and rings;
- a nylon shank with a thirty-inch chain;
- a four-foot, untasseled dressage whip;
- at least six poles, twelve feet long;
- two sheets of plastic, approximately three by twelve feet, clear or white.

To set up a complete course for one or more horses, you'll need in addition to the above
- eight barrels;
- one bridge or seesaw;
- ten more poles twelve feet long;
- twigs and branches;
- several automobile tires;
- jump standards from which to hang the plastic sheets.

A typical course of ground obstacles is pictured in figure 47. In the background we've laid tires flat on the ground; next to these is a collection of oil drums or barrels; a three-by-nine-foot board simulates a bridge; to the right is a plastic archway to go under; in the middle is the labyrinth, and in the foreground is the grid. The exercises should be varied from day to day and the course can be arranged differently to maintain the horse's interest.

Fig. 47

## BASIC GROUND EXERCISES

### Teaching Your Horse to Stand

The first lesson you'll be asking your horse to learn in your T.E.A.M. program is to stand quietly while tied, whether he is alone or near other horses, whom he may not kick out at.

We might add that he should stand in a mannerly fashion, not pawing or moving about, nor tossing his head or chewing on anything within reach, including the lead rope. A horse is often required to stand quietly, but how do you teach him to stand so that he really complies?

Unhurried, quiet, thorough training is necessary to teach a horse to stand without requiring you to resort to punishment. The horse would not understand being punished in this context at all, for in his natural habitat he'd never have to stand still, except when it suited him. Even horses who live their entire lives in a stall will not know how to stand on demand until they've been taught. Nevertheless, we assume that when we put a halter on a horse and tie him somewhere, he will stand quietly as a matter of course.

How very important this first lesson is, yet how few people recognize its importance. Your horse will learn discipline and patience. He'll also learn most easily in the company of other horses. Military and police horses stand tied outside for hours, an important requirement for horses who must obey the slightest perceptible command totally without resistance, but they are almost always among other horses. Many horses can't stand quietly. They paw, dance about, and call out to other horses. Try to ride them away from the barn and their stable mates and they throw a fit.

About 50 percent of the horses we describe in this book were of the oversensitive variety. They needed to have handlers work with them, doing body work until they learned to stand quietly on the lead and dropped their heads in response to the quiet pressure of the handlers' hands (see figures 19 and 20). It was then much easier and safer to teach them to stand tied quietly and patiently.

In all work with your horse, his and your safety must remain of primary importance. You need a correctly fitted halter made of leather or nylon. (A rope halter won't work.) The noseband should sit about three fingers' width below the horse's protruding cheekbone and should be loose enough for him to chew comfortably, yet not be so loose that he could get his foot caught in it. The rings must be large enough to allow a chain to pass easily through them (figures 48 and 49). Given a choice, we prefer working with nylon halters as leather ones break more easily and are harder to keep clean.

Decide where you want to tie your horse. It should be a place where he isn't afraid to be, somewhere where he can see and hear his stable mates and where he won't be able to hurt himself. *Never* tie your horse to barbed wire or the rails of a fence; tie only to something really well anchored. Make sure no wire is lying about that he might get his foot stuck in. In the beginning he is likely to move around a little. Thus, if you tie to a wall, make sure there are no protruding nails or hooks within the radius of his body; nor should wheelbarrows or other equipment be parked in this area.

Having taken all precautions to ensure your horse's safety, you must nonetheless realize that you can't train through gentleness alone. You will

Fig. 48                                              Fig. 49

need to use those tools that will enable you to communicate in a clear, brief, and specific way. In the T.E.A.M. method we use a nylon lead with a thirty-inch chain for the nose (figures 48–50) and a four-foot-long stiff whip, which we call a "wand."*

Be sure the chain is thirty inches long. A chain that is too short (see figure 50) cannot reach to the upper side ring of the halter and still leave approximately six to eight inches of slack (figure 51). Ideally, the lead attached to the chain should measure about six feet. Again, be sure your horse's halter fits well. If the halter does not fit the horse well, the effect of the signal on the chain will be diminished.

If the horse is to be led from the left, the end of the chain is passed through the lower halter ring on the left side, looped once around the nose band (figure 48), passed through the lower ring on the right, and then hooked onto the upper ring on the right (figure 49). For leading from the right, which should definitely be done from time to time, the chain is run in the same way, but from right to left.

This chain is not intended as a tool of punishment. It is used for the immediate, yet short, effect it exerts on the horse's nose. In most cases the horse will become more obedient as soon as you put the chain on.

There are five important points to remember when using the chain:

---

*This equipment can be ordered from T.E.A.M. headquarters. Ordering information can be found on the back page of this book.

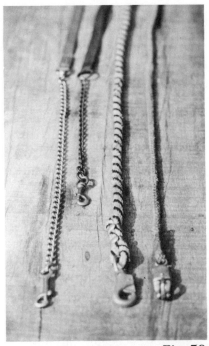

Fig. 50                     Fig. 51

1. *Never* tie a horse with a lead chain. Should he pull back, the pressure on his nose would be too strong. If you want to use the chain to correct misbehavior while he's learning to stand tied, tie him with a regular lead and hold the chain lead in your hand (see figure 48).

2. Hold the chain at about the height of the horse's cheekbone so that you'll be able to use the chain simply by moving your wrist.

3. The effect of the chain should always be to reinforce a concept, not to punish your horse or instill fear. It will take some practice before you become proficient with its use. From the beginning, though, impress upon yourself the basic precept that you should not put continuous pressure on the chain, whether you're standing or leading. This is not because the chain would cause the horse pain, but because it would soon lose all its effectiveness. It is common to see a person dragging their reluctant horse along behind them or hanging back on the lead rope of a horse who's forging impatiently ahead.

4. In the T.E.A.M. work the lead chain is almost always used in conjunction with the wand (see pages 57–62). It is the addition and use of the wand to signal the horse to stay back that teaches a horse to respond to the subtle signals with the chain as opposed to the imprecise communication from a pull on a lead rope.

5. Should your horse panic and run backwards, go with him until

he stops. If you pull back in the moment the horse is running backwards he could flip over and be seriously injured. On the other hand, if you go with him in the first few seconds of panic he'll stop on his own. If a horse is difficult, work him in an enclosed area.

This entire training method, with each step of the process depicted in great detail, is designed to help you avoid fighting with your horse and to make working with the horse something that even the amateur horse owner can do correctly and safely. It's also designed, of course, to produce a friendly horse who's eager to learn, a horse who won't lose his spirit or personality in the course of training, but who will gain manners in the bargain.

Following each lesson, remember to reward your horse with a stroke on the neck and some words of praise.

In teaching your horse to stand, you should stay close to him and correct him if he paws with a stroke or tap on the legs and a reminding word to stand quietly. Don't just tie him up somewhere and then leave thinking, "He'll get used to it."

If, instead, you slowly and patiently *show* your horse what he is to do, he will learn several useful things from this lesson:

> He'll learn that you're expecting something specific from him and he'll learn exactly what that is, namely, that he is to stand quietly. Whenever he does something wrong, you'll be there to correct him. This will enable him to learn this basic but difficult lesson correctly from the very beginning. As a result, he will soon be able to perform what's required of him. He'll also learn to appreciate your presence and the work being done on his body.

This first standing lesson can soon be combined with grooming, but keep in mind that the primary goal of the lesson remains teaching the horse to stand quietly. For this reason, be gentle in your grooming. Don't be rough. If the horse gets nervous or regresses at all in his previously learned lesson of standing still, you'll need to make sure that your grooming isn't hurting him anywhere. Go over his entire body with a soft brush or cloth and try to determine the spot at which he becomes restless. Perhaps you've discovered a small wound? Or maybe you've been too rough? Many horses, especially the thin-skinned types, are very sensitive to being groomed. Others, it seems, you could clean with a wire brush without their minding. However insignificant the irritation may be, however, you'll need to pay attention to it because your horse won't be able to stand as long as he feels threatened.

*Once you've succeeded in conquering your horse's resistance and have taught him to stand, he's on his way to quietly obeying you when you ask him to do other things contrary to his nature.*

### Teaching Your Horse to Accept the Wand

Another indispensable tool for training your horse is a four-foot-long, stiff dressage whip, which we call a "wand." It should be smooth and un-tasseled, and should have a thickened handle with a knob at the end. This wand is an extension of your arm. It indicates direction and calls the horse to attention. It is a helpful tool, rarely used to punish. For this reason, the horse should have no fear of the wand. With the aid of the wand, the handler is able to control the horse from a distance in more advanced lessons. Like the chain and complementing its effect, the wand teaches the horse to react promptly to subtle but clear signals.

To accustom your horse to the wand, thread the chain through the halter as we've described and hold the shank of the lead in one hand. If your horse is very apprehensive, get an assistant to hold him and offer him some oats in a flat container.

Many horses have an inexplicable fear of the whip (figure 52), even when, to our knowledge, they've never been hit by one. These horses usually are oversensitive to touch per se. They will move away from the mere touch of the hand, tend to be cinchy, and are usually nervous. It is best to try to teach such a horse that the wand is not to be feared by holding the lesson in an enclosed area where he feels comfortable.

**Fig. 52**

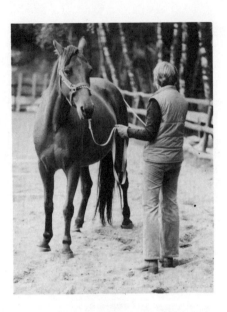

**Fig. 53**

Take the wand in your right hand, show it to your horse, and then begin to stroke it gently along his whole body (figure 53). Gentleness is very important in this lesson as it is vital that your horse not perceive the wand as an implement of punishment. Start where he is least threatened.

If he kicks out at the wand at first (figure 52), just ignore it. Talk quietly and encouragingly to him while you continue to try to get him to accept the touch of the wand. Hold the lead relatively slack and let him move around you for the first few minutes, reassuring him with your voice if he's really nervous.

You'll readily see if your previous work has been thorough enough. A horse who has learned to let you explore his body with your hands, who finds your touch pleasant, who stands well while being groomed, and who has learned to obey the least warning of the chain will also learn to accept the wand in a few sessions. On your part, this seemingly simple work will require a degree of self-discipline, quiet patience, and clear understanding of purpose, namely:

> The horse is to learn to allow foreign objects to touch his body and not run from them in fear. He is to allow himself to be touched even in sensitive places such as on his hind legs, under his belly, on the udder or sheath, and on his head and ears.

He'll get better each time you work with him as a result of his own satisfaction at having understood the lesson, having performed it successfully, and having been praised for it.

The horse should soon calmly allow the wand to gently stroke his body. If he moves, you should patiently move him back to the spot he was in. He'll soon stand perfectly still. You can then proceed to the next lesson.

**Fig. 54**

Take a step away from your horse and from this new distance stroke him again along his whole body with the wand, touching him on his front legs, his belly (figure 54), between his hind legs, and on his croup. With encouraging words, move now around the entire horse in as large a circle as the lead will allow. If he makes any attempt to move away, give a short pull and release on the chain to inhibit him, reinforced with a quieting command to "Staaaand."

With encouragement, your horse will in a very short time stand quietly on a loose lead and allow you to move around his body without his paying the least attention to the wand's presence.

You now have a horse who no longer moves away any time he feels something strange touch his body. Not only does he stand, but he waits patiently to see what's to happen next.

This lesson could be important in your riding—if, for example, your horse gets a long twig caught between his legs, in his tail, or under his belly; or if he steps into some wire or bumps into an electric fence used to cordon off a pasture; or if the girth or driving harness breaks.

With the following exercises, you'll expand the use of the wand immensely. Depending on where you use it, it will tell your horse:

Fig. 55

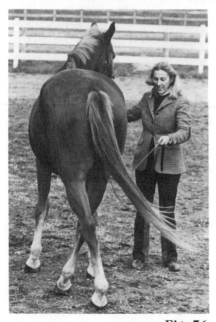

Fig. 56

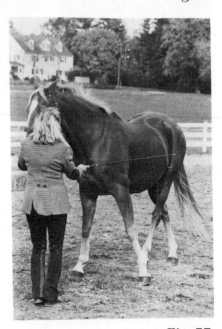

Fig. 57

- to move a given foot back under him (figure 55);
- to move forward or backward;
- to execute a turn on the forehand (figure 56);
- to move sideways (figure 57).

To prepare your horse for turns, you need to teach him two ways of moving sideways. First you will teach him to turn on his forehand. In this exercise he must move his hind legs around his front legs. Stand at his head looking towards his tail and tap with the wand against the side of the hind leg you want him to cross in front of the other (figure 56). At the same time, with the other hand stabilize the horse's head with your hand on the chain two or three inches from the halter ring so you don't pull the head to the side. Then repeat the exercise in the other direction.

Next you'll ask your horse to move sideways. To do this, tap so the wand taps flat against the shoulder and the barrel simultaneously. Then hold the wand flat against his side (figure 57). Each time the horse completes a sideways step, let him stop and think about what he's just accomplished before moving on to the next step.

With practice you will find the wand is an indispensable means of communication between horse and handler. Throughout this book we've included photographs demonstrating its many different uses. For example, you can use its handle to keep an as-yet-unschooled horse at a

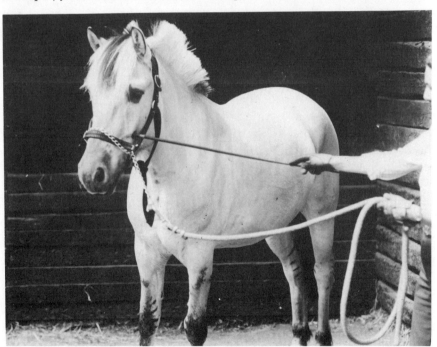

Fig. 58

distance (figure 58). It is a natural extension of your own hand and arm. Do not wave it around, but instead learn to use it flexibly as the situation demands. The greater dexterity you develop with the wand, the more success you'll have with it. In the sections to come that describe the ground exercises, we'll include specific directions on the use of the wand.

### Teaching Your Horse to Lead

Leading looks so easy. Everybody does it. However, the manner in which you lead your horse determines if he will respect and obey your subtlest signals. Once a horse learns to pull against you, he's going to be less sensitive under saddle to the direction of your aids. If, on the other hand, you teach your horse to react to the lightest of signals without fear and if you develop his trust through reward, you'll be well on your way to having a well-behaved horse. Whether you lead him or he leads you will relate to his obedience under saddle. An advantage of all this attention to detail is that this training method can be successfully employed by anybody with a basic sensitivity towards other living beings. You don't need to be a polished rider in order to train your horse in hand to be well-behaved and pleasant.

Figure 59 demonstrates the basic leading position. Take the end of the chain in your right hand and the wand and the end of the shank in your left. Stand with your shoulder even with your horse's head. Keep your arm extended in order to teach your horse to maintain a distance of about two and a half to three feet from you. First ask him to move forward with a voice command to "walk" and a short (three-second) pull and release with the chain.

The most difficult aspect of all work in hand is, in fact, learning to use your hands correctly. Every minute change in your hand's position has a meaning affecting your horse in a specific way and eliciting different results. For most work, hold your hand at the height of the lower halter ring, not any lower. With your hand held at this height, your own body will be in balance. Don't pull your horse's head toward you as it won't allow him to move or halt straight.

Your hand should be held at the height of the lower halter ring and the chain should have a little slack when you're not signaling. Hold the end of the lead and the wand in your outside hand, grasping the wand in the middle with the butt end upward.

Your body position is also immensely important. We call the body positions assumed for the T.E.A.M. program "body language." This means the horse understands the changes in your position as a specific language that tells him directly and exactly what he is supposed to do.

For example, if you walk straight ahead parallel to your horse, you signal to him also to walk straight. To stop him, you move your body in a single decisive step at an angle towards his head. We'll come back to this use of body language in our examples throughout the book.

Walk next to your horse's head so that you have him in sight and he can see you. If you walk at his shoulder, the horse has too much of a jump on you if he suddenly bolts forward.

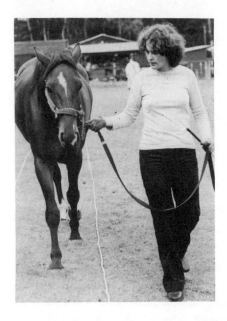

Fig. 59

**Halting.** Getting your horse to halt in balance is our goal. To achieve this you need four signals. You'll combine them at first, but later any single one will suffice.

1. Your low voice tells him softly, "Whoa."
2. Your hand gives a now-familiar pull and release on the chain.
3. Your outside hip and shoulder turn inward towards him, creating a blocking effect.
4. You move the butt end of the wand up and down about two feet in front of his nose. (If you hold it too close, he won't be able to see the movement and interpret its meaning correctly.)

With your outside shoulder turned slightly in front of your horse and the wand in front of his nose, you're in a good position to control any situation. If he gets excited at this point, you can step away from him, giving him a longer lead, and you'll still be in a position to react.

In asking for the halt, continue to hold your hand at the height of the

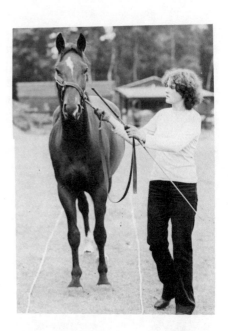

**Fig. 60**

lower halter ring (the handler pictured in figure 60 has her hand held too low). Once your horse has come to a halt and is attentive, you must relax the chain slightly. In this way the chain will hang a bit loosely again as soon as the horse halts. You'll need a little practice and constant attention to the position of your hands to perfect this technique. With experience, your signals will become increasingly lighter and your own overall balance will improve. (The ropes shown in this photo have been laid in parallel lines to indicate to the handler if she is leading in a truly straight line and if she's maintaining an equal distance from her horse.)

**Trotting on the lead.**   Once your horse is moving forward freely and is halting promptly, you can ask him to trot. To do this, use the voice signal "Tee-rot!" and give him a light tap with the wand on the top of the croup. Your horse should walk, trot, and halt on command and in balance. With each practice session he will obey your signals better and better until the mere body language of bringing your outside shoulder inward, for example, or taking your hand back will be enough to cause him to slow down or halt.

Even with the best of training, your horse could startle when you begin running next to him at the trot. Here your best aid is a helper. Standing off to the side and a little to the rear, this helper should ask the horse to trot on while you run next to him, reassuring him with your voice. Be sure the helper is far enough to the side not to be kicked if the horse feels threatened.

**Reinforcing "Whoa."**   We'll now add another exercise to reinforce your horse's response to the command "Whoa." Immediately *after he stops*, thump his chest once with the butt end of the wand—firmly but not enough to hurt. The first time you do this, your horse might jump forward. Should this happen, thump him again. As you thump him say "Whoa," and after you thump him, stroke him several times with the wand to reassure him. Most horses will step back the second time you thump. If he still doesn't understand you may be thumping too lightly or you may need to go to another lesson and then come back to this one.

This thumping reorganizes your horse's nervous system's response to fear stimuli. A horse's automatic reaction to fear is to run forward. Even if his rider uses the bit to slow him down, he'll duck his head to avoid the pain and just try to go faster. This exercise teaches him to respond in a new way in that he now steps back instead of rushing forward. Later, when you say "Whoa" from the saddle, he'll respond promptly.

Soon you'll be able to lay the lead over your horse's neck and allow him to walk freely next to you (figure 61). He'll now react promptly, coming to a halt at your subtlest signals—raising your hand or a soft "Whoa." And again, without a lot of trouble, you've trained your horse to work with you gladly, because he has understood what you wanted, could perform as you asked, and received praise for his performance. In the last few days he'll have gotten quieter and more trusting; at the same time his intelligence will have been stimulated and he will be more alert.

Fig. 61

Leading the horse correctly is so fundamental to all of the ground exercises we are about to introduce that we want to describe a few other basic methods of leading and point out the mistakes people often make when leading horses.

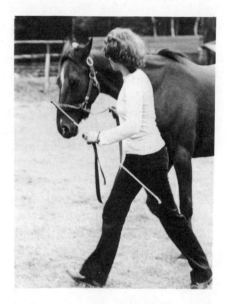

**Fig. 62**

To lead your horse away from you around a turn, you'll again be giving the signal with your body. Move one step forward and in towards him, somewhat blocking his way. At the same time point the butt end of the whip to the right in front of his nose (figure 62). Your horse should follow these two gentle signals without resistance.

The position of your body is of immense importance. Whether you lead your horse from a position by his head or back by his shoulder makes a major difference in balance and response to subtle signals. Many horses haven't learned to move in a straight line because so often they are pulled to the left by normal leading methods. They tend, instead, to drift in towards the trainer. This is especially the case with very strong or nervous horses who pull a lot. To slow down the horse, usually the trainer leans in to him or pokes his elbow into the horse's neck (figure 63). Bending the horse around us in this way does work but it puts them off balance and teaches them to pull against us.

One five-foot-tall lady weighing about 108 pounds described how her seventeen-hand Thoroughbred would run people over on purpose, could not be controlled at horse shows, and bucked under saddle. Every time she took him out of his stall, he'd drag her along dangling under his neck where he couldn't even *see* her any more. The simple leading exercises we've described above changed him in a few days. Dutch, the horse pic-

**Fig. 63**                                    **Fig. 64**

tured in 63–65, presented a similar case, which we'll describe later in detail (see pages 122–136).

The simplest way to lead a horse safely and in balance is pictured in figure 64. Horse and handler move in balance independently of each other. The handler's right hand is at the height of the lower halter ring, which also ensures that he doesn't unconsciously pull the horse towards him. The wand is held to reinforce the distance between him and the horse so that it can be brought easily in front of the horse's head to slow him down with minimal use of the chain. In this way, the horse soon learns to walk next to the handler, controlling his own speed in response to the signal from the wand. These simple exercises improve the horse's sense of balance.

Our next photo (figure 65) looks much better, but the handler is about one step too far back. To stop correctly from this position, he should be even with his horse's nose to be able to signal with the whip

**Fig. 65**

for the halt. If he's not able to do this, he'll have to pull on the lead, which, in turn, will pull the horse's nose to the inside and block the handler's path.

**Leading from the Right.** Leading from the right is an important exercise for both horse and handler. Many horses under saddle are stiff to the right. You'll often hear the explanation that this comes from the way the horse was positioned in its dam's womb. Our theory is that this results from being led, saddled, and mounted from the left.

Many horses have trouble being longed to the right. They're stiff in this direction and go much better to the left. We notice quite the opposite, however, with imported Islandic ponies; in Iceland horses are led and mounted from the right.

To make a horse more elastic and supple, all T.E.A.M. exercises should be done both from the left and right. This is especially important with the leading exercises (figure 66).

In leading from the right, the chain is threaded from the right: first through the lower halter ring on the right side, then once around the noseband, then through the lower ring on the left and fastened to the upper ring on that side.

**Fig. 66**

The horse's brain works as ours does in that it directs right- and left-hand activities from different parts of the brain. Everything we teach a horse from the right will be a new task with new effects on the brain.

To help equalize any awkward movement on the part of either horse or handler from this new angle, it is best to hold the lead a bit longer than normal. If your horse has learned to lead well from the left, he will soon lead freely and independently from the right as well.

**Leading Between Two Hands.** Your horse has learned to lead and to stand quietly. He knows to wait patiently for something new and interesting to begin. He is now going to learn to move forward in response to a light tap with the wand on the croup. To teach this, you'll change your position. Stand to the left of your horse holding the lead in your left hand and the wand in your right. Standing like this will enable you to see where you're touching the horse with the wand as well as the horse's reaction to it. Your left hand should be closer to his nose than to his shoulder (figure 67). To move your horse forward, give him the familiar signals from voice and chain and tap him lightly on the top of his croup. If your horse should jump forward, steady him with your left hand on the lead shank at the triangle on the end of the chain.

If your horse doesn't move forward from several taps, don't punish him by hitting him harder. He may not understand the tap as a signal. Simply encourage him to move forward by applying pressure with the chain in your left hand as you tap him with the wand in your right hand.

Fig. 67

Figure 68 also illustrates working the horse between two hands. This method impresses the signal of the wand clearly to the horse. We often use the position between two hands when we first ask the horse to trot on the lead, and it's always used when working on the short longe (see figure 72) and for teaching the horse to load.

As with tying and leading, you should do this work between two hands from both sides. From the right, the lead is held in the right hand, the wand in the left, and the chain, of course, is threaded from the right.

**Fig. 68**

Because the horse's eyes are positioned on the side of his head, he will see many things quite differently from one side to the other. This means that any action that he is used to seeing from the left may be surprising when seen from the right. For this reason it is of the utmost importance that you pay attention to both sides of the horse in his training and change back and forth often.

One further point on working the horse between two hands: your horse can see your whole body from this position. He's going to notice every change in your position and interpret these changes. In other words, he'll "listen" exactly to what we've termed your body language.

Our goal is for the horse to move straight at a distance of from two to six feet from the handler. To make the lesson easier it is best to gradually increase the distance, particularly when trotting.

The wand plays an important role. It maintains the correct distance between horse and handler and prevents the horse from moving out in front. This technique is shown in figure 69. The handler moves her hand with the wand up and towards the horse's head while her outside shoulder moves to block his forward motion. The horse interprets her body language and the use of the wand correctly and stops. His ears are attentive and he's obviously a little unsure of what he has done wrong. The handler then quiets the horse with her voice and gently directs his head straight. With the command "Walk," she'll move the wand back again to encourage forward movement.

Fig. 69

The horse will soon learn to comply with your commands if you've praised him each time. Up to this point, he has learned
- to go forward to a signal from the wand and your spoken command, "Walk";
- to pay attention to your body language;
- to go forward from a signal on the chain.

Of course, he'll learn all this if you lead standing next to him as well, but the importance of the work between two hands will become apparent in the following chapters. It serves many purposes:

- It's the first step in teaching a horse to longe;
- it helps in loading;
- it is an indispensable aid for teaching the horse to stand for mounting;
- it will always be useful whenever the horse refuses to go somewhere like over a small ditch or past some fearsome object.

Figure 70 demonstrates another way of using the wand to move a horse forward at the walk or trot. In this position, the handler holds the lead in her right hand, the wand in her left. She's concentrating on teaching her young horse to move forward freely at the walk (actually, it would be better if she held the end of the shank in her left hand along with the wand to enable her to slide her right hand closer to the chain as necessary). The wand is held just under the handle, leaving it long enough to be able to reach around the handler's back and touch the horse's quarters. If she wants to signal "halt," the handler can move the butt end further up in her hand in order to be able to hold it in front of her horse's head or tap him on the chest—two signals to halt.

This will take some practice. Often the handler is concentrating so

**Fig. 70**

much on what's happening up front that he is surprised when the horse suddenly jumps forward at the tap of the wand. Obviously it was too strong a tap or hit the wrong place. Also, in the beginning most people find it awkward to tap the wand from the left around their backs. Here, too, you may find it useful to have a helper to observe and direct you.

We use this method only rarely for several reasons.

1. The handler cannot see exactly where he is touching the horse with the wand, so the horse is often surprised.
2. The horse does not respond with awareness since he can't see where the signal is coming from.
3. This position puts the handler back by the shoulder—a position to be avoided for previously stated reasons.

However, there are situations where this position can be most effective. For example, when you're teaching a horse to trot without the assistance of a helper.

Once your horse moves forward to the tap of the wand you will be spared many a difficult time in later training. Your horse has been praised for his efforts, and his interest in other work has been awakened.

All the T.E.A.M. exercises described thus far are required work for all horses. Even when we don't mention it specifically from now on, it is assumed that all work in hand begins with

- standing quietly tied;
- work with the wand;
- leading;
- work between two hands.

Whether you choose to use all or only some of the exercises that follow depends mainly on your horse and his individual problems, as well as on the time at your disposal and how much of it you want to invest in your horse.

## FURTHERING YOUR HORSE'S EDUCATION

### *Longeing Your Horse on the Short Line*

Longeing on the short line—the normal lead shank—aims at making your horse more supple on curved lines and at teaching him to follow commands given at a greater distance than you've been from him while leading. He'll need to halt in response to the word "Whoa" and the movement of the wand in front of his face (figure 71). He'll also need to pick up the walk or trot from voice command or in response to a tap from the wand—and to quicken or slow down the pace of these gaits on command. Basically, this longeing is an enhancement of the work you did between two hands. It will teach the horse to stride forward freely, relaxed and stretching his neck low. It also teaches him to wait patiently for your next command without becoming anxious or tugging on the line. If he's been taught to lead from the left and the right and has been worked as described between two hands, he should be able to learn this lesson in about ten minutes.

Many horses are driven about with a longe whip on a long line reacting from fear rather than from understanding. It's not unusual for a young, anxious, or simply disobedient horse to plunge around on the twenty-five-foot longe totally out of control. The new horse owner or a handler who's not very strong or skillful is probably all too familiar with this rather precarious situation.

Fig. 71

Our goal here is for the horse to move quietly around as the handler walks in a circle (or preferably, an oval) at a radius of at least ten feet so the horse's circle is not too small (figure 72a). To start, play the lead shank out slowly until you have the end in your hand. Then ask your horse to move forward by tapping him on the top of the croup with the wand.

To maintain a *walk*, use a voice command and point the wand at a spot just about at his hock. To signal *trot* say "Trot!" and raise the wand a bit higher. Raise the wand above his croup to further increase the pace (figure 72b).

At the trot you can widen the circle a bit more by walking in a larger circle. This will considerably widen the outer circle on which the horse is traveling.

To slow your horse, use a long, low voice command to "Walk" or "Whoa" and bring the wand in front of his head (see figure 71).

Don't ask your horse to canter on this small circle. You'll have accomplished your goal once he responds to your voice commands at the walk or trot.

**Fig. 72a**

**Fig. 72b**

If necessary, ask a helper to lead the horse around you from the outside until he stays out on the circle and accepts your commands.

To longe from either the left or the right without having to change the chain, run it through the two lower rings and around the horse's nose and fasten it under his chin (figure 73).

**Fig. 73**

### *The Labyrinth*

The labyrinth is made out of six jump poles about twelve feet in length. It should be laid out as in figure 77. When you later ride through it, make it larger. In this maze, your horse will be required to execute a series of bends to the right and to the left. Between the bends he'll need to go straight and must halt on command from any position. To accomplish all this he'll need to move through slowly, step by step, concentrating fully on what he's doing.

Horses learn many different things from this exercise. Nervous horses learn that they do better when they go slower and pay exact attention to the signals of their handler. Lazy, disinterested horses grow more alert, paying attention to subtle signals of the wand and the trainer's body. Horses who fear the wand soon learn to accept it. They begin to understand that it is never there to hurt them but is there to help them understand the exercise. Without the rider's weight on their backs, uncoordinated horses improve their balance and stiff horses learn to relax and bend supply around the poles.

There are three basic techniques of working through the labyrinth.

1.  The first time, lead your horse in the normal position with your

right hand grasping the chain end of the lead and your left hand holding the other end and the wand (figure 74). Walk your horse quietly through once just to familiarize him with the poles and strange pattern. Keep your hand at the height of the lower halter ring and stretch it a little towards him to maintain a distance—he's going to need room to see where he's going.

**Fig. 74**

Practice taking slow and shortened steps in the labyrinth. Horses mirror what we do instinctively, and you'll find if *you* walk slowly, your horse will too. The slower you can get him to do an exercise, the more he'll think about what he's doing.

The horse probably won't have any problems until he reaches the first bend, where he has only a small space in which to turn his body (see figure 74). You'll need to give him time to organize his feet. The sharp turns of the labyrinth encourage him to think about where his legs are and what he needs to do with them. Our aim is to have the hind feet follow the track of the front feet. He has to think specifically about where to put each leg—a process that is new to him.

Most horses become perceptively more alert as they negotiate this maze. If your horse gets "stuck" on a turn and can't decide what to do, tap the leg he needs to move next with your wand. If he steps out of the labyrinth in a corner, don't punish him; just bring him back in and continue. However he's positioned, bring the wand forward and hold it about one and a half feet from his face to signal "halt." You may have to walk outside the labyrinth to give him more room. After a while you'll find that your horse's movements through the labyrinth will become light and balanced (figure 75).

Once he can negotiate the labyrinth in a totally relaxed fashion, you can vary the pattern.

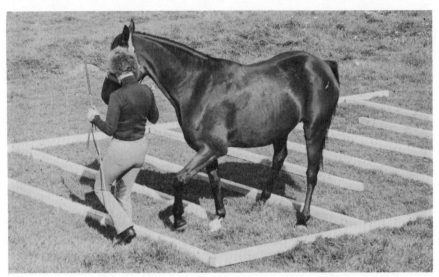

Fig. 75

2. In this next phase the horse will learn to concentrate and obey your slightest signal. He must be observant of your body language and concentrate in a way that ensures relaxation rather than tension. In this way he'll learn to be patient and remain alert at the same time.

As soon as you enter the labyrinth, turn around to face your horse (figure 76). Stand about two feet in front of him and hold the lead shank in your right hand about one to two feet from the end of the chain. In your left hand hold the end of the lead and the middle of the wand, which you should cross in front of you. Back through the labyrinth having your horse follow you step by step with slow, short steps. Halt after each or every other step and wait about fifteen seconds before proceeding. To signal for your horse to move forward, your right hand, held as usual at about the height of the lower halter ring, gives the chain a slight pull and release; to halt your horse, your left hand moves the wand toward his nose with a blocking gesture or fanning back and forth like a slow wind-shield wiper. The first few times you ask him to stop it might be necessary to tap lightly with the butt end of the wand on his noseband or on the chain. Once he stands still, give him a rub on the nose so that he understands that the tap wasn't meant as a punishment. Most horses learn after about three trips through the labyrinth to move forward or halt at the slightest signal from you.

Perhaps by now you can see how important such an exercise can be for your work under saddle. A nervous, tense horse will learn to wait for fine signals from the rein and leg aids. By teaching him a number of new signals, you're giving him more information to work with and learn from. He'll gradually come to understand that he needs to wait for a signal from you, no matter what that signal might be. A lazy, uninterested horse will become more alert through this exercise.

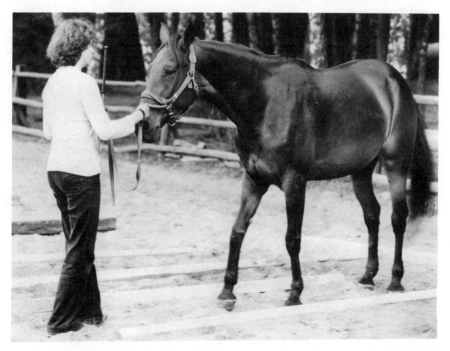

**Fig. 76**

3. Your next effort will be to get your horse to listen more to the signals of the wand. Use the position *between two hands* (figure 77). Looking at your horse, hold the end of the chain with the entire lead in your left hand. Hold the wand in your right hand. To enter the labyrinth, rest the wand lightly on your horse's croup. He should wait patiently for a signal to walk on. Lift the wand slightly and give him a light tap. At the same time, still facing him, give a quiet pull and release with the chain to move him forward. After two or three steps, signal for him to halt by bringing the wand in front of his chest and giving a gentle pull and release on the chain. Tapping on the croup for "forward" and on the chest for

"halt" are new signals for his nervous system and activate new brain cells. His brain thus develops an expanded ability to learn. This exercise will teach a nervous horse to relax and a "lazy" horse to pay more attention and to react more quickly to your signals.

**Fig. 77**

When negotiating the turns, change your position to the side the horse is turning toward. The lead and wand then change hands. Hold the lead in your left hand and the wand in your right hand to elicit bends to the left and change them to the opposite hands for bends to the right.

Don't punish your horse if he blunders through the corners of the labyrinth, stepping on the poles. If necessary, straighten the poles again. The next time, before you get to the first corner, lift your horse's head somewhat to help balance him. This will cause him to carry more of his weight over his hindquarters, which will lighten the forehand and enable him to better alter the height of his next step, in midstride, if necessary.

As we have stressed with all the T.E.A.M. exercises, these bending exercises should also be practiced leading from the right as well as from the left.

You won't need to drill these exercises. If you work your horse through the labyrinth five or six times each day for several days, he'll have learned a lot. He'll have learned a new way of organizing the movement of his legs, to think for himself, and to concentrate; at the same time, he'll have developed a better sense of balance.

Riding through the labyrinth is an excellent way to reinforce your horse's newly won coordination. It will also make the training of all further bending from the saddle easier (figure 78). Sit exactly in the middle of the saddle and move your weight to the outside seat bone in the

Fig. 78

curves (in the photo shown, this should be the rider's left seat bone). This will make it easier for your horse to move his inside hind foot. It is quite clear in this photo how the previous in-hand exercises have improved the suppleness of this horse.

### Teaching Your Horse to Back

Many people seem to find it difficult to teach their horses to back. A horse's instinct doesn't tell him to back up. As an animal of flight, his natural reflexes push him either forward or sideways in escape.

Teaching him to back from the ground is quite simple.

Grasp the chain in your left hand at the spot where it comes out of the halter, in other words, not at the usual place where the chain connects to the lead. Now, bending your right thumb slightly and letting the other fingers of your right hand rest on the horse's shoulder, push your thumb against the point of his shoulder. *Pressure on this spot triggers a reflex response which causes the horse to back up* (figure 79). As you push, say "Baaack," quietly but distinctly, and lift his head a bit with your left hand. By lifting his head, you cause the horse to shift more weight onto his haunches, lightening his forehand and enabling him to back with ease.

Press, then release, repeating the process if necessary, giving the voice command "Baaack" each time. Reinforce these signals by pulling back very lightly on the chain and then releasing so he will also respond

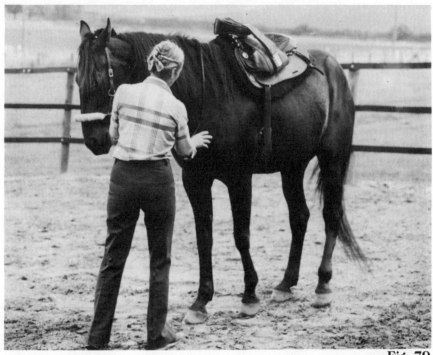

**Fig. 79**

to the rein aid and voice from under saddle. Few horses fail to respond to this combination of pressure and voice command. Soon he'll back correctly and easily.

Don't ask your horse to back more than three steps at a time. After practicing two or three times, stop the exercise and praise him by stroking his legs with the wand.

Once your horse has correctly followed your signal to back a few times, give a light pull and release with the chain, asking him to "baaack." This time, however, also tap the wand lightly against his chest with your other hand. Again, ask for only a few steps, and don't overpractice. When he's understood this new signal, tap on his foot instead of on his chest (figure 80). Tap until he moves his foot back, then tap on the other foot. With each variation in the command, the horse learns more and faster and begins to differentiate what your signals mean.

To reiterate: the horse can't back if his weight is on his forehand. Thus, you'll lighten his forehand by slightly lifting his head. This will be necessary both in backing and in teaching lateral movements.

The first time you try backing your horse from the saddle, have a helper on the ground give the now well-known signals. In this way your horse will learn to back easily, even with your weight in the saddle. Once this works, you can then lean forward a little a tap him with your wand

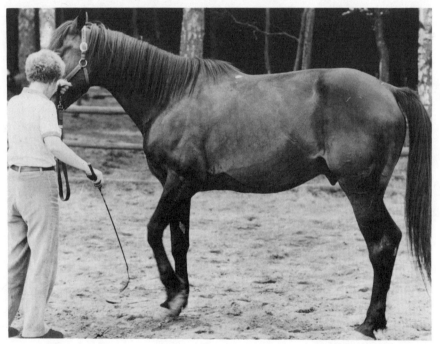

Fig. 80

on his chest, while you take and release on the rein. You'll be able to dispense with the wand altogether after a few more lessons and soon thereafter you won't need to give the voice command any more either. A simple squeeze and release of the rein or shift of your weight in the saddle will suffice.

It's important that you not overpractice backing either in hand or under saddle. Horses learn much faster than we realize and can become resistant and bored if a lesson is repeated too often.

### The L

For this exercise, place two pairs of jump poles on the ground at right angles, leaving a four-foot channel between the poles (figure 81). This obstacle can be used for a variety of exercises, both backing up and moving straight forward. It can also be used for lateral work, and the half turn on the forehand can be practiced around its corner. The rather narrow path of the L teaches your horse to work with discipline and coordination.

A basic principle of continued importance here is that you not lose your patience or get upset if your horse doesn't understand what you

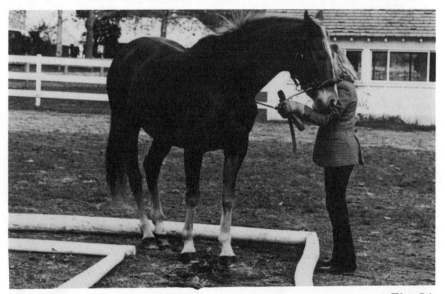

**Fig. 81**

want him to do at first and consequently performs the exercise badly. The cause of his confusion can be that you haven't thought specifically enough about how to teach him the exercise, or that your signals are mixed or unclear.

Start by walking your horse slowly through the L so that he can take a good look at it. In the beginning, many horses can't estimate the height of the border poles, nor how far away from their hoofs the poles lie. Thus the L is a useful tool for helping the horse learn to estimate strange obstacles accurately that he otherwise might fear.

The second time through, lead your horse just to the turn and then back him out again. Use the butt end of the wand to direct his legs, tapping the front of each leg as you want him to move it.

Next, lead him through and around the turn, then ask him to back to the turn. To help your horse negotiate the turn backwards, tap with the light end of the wand against his side and ask him to take two steps turning around the forehand. Now back up two more steps. Next ask him to move his front legs through the turn, directing them sideways with your wand. You're now through the turn and can continue to back straight to the end.

Should your horse step over a pole, don't punish him. That's going to happen from time to time. Walk him forward a few steps and quiet and encourage him with a friendly word before asking him to try again. *The learning process itself is more important than immediate successful performance.* If your horse has understood the earlier exercises, it won't take him long to grasp this one either.

Teaching your horse in hand to move sideways from pressure of the wand on his side is going to make his learning the necessary coordination for later lateral movements under saddle seem effortless. Attach the chain as shown in figure 73 so that it won't pull his head to the side. To move him to the right, stand to his left, parallel to his nose, facing his tail. Hold your left hand on his halter. Now press the entire length of the wand against his side (not just the point of the wand as he would confuse this with a sign to move his haunches sideways). Tap the wand lightly against his side and move your own body left, pushing his head left as you move, without making him crooked (figure 81). Once he is moving sideways easily, position him in the L so that he has the outside pole between his front and hind feet (figure 82). Ask him to move a few steps to

Fig. 82

the right and then a few steps back again to the left. Many horses can't calculate the height of the poles from this position and will be afraid to step over them. If you stand in the middle of the L, on either side of the horse, you'll find it easy to ask your horse to move sideways in either direction. This exercise is often required in trail classes and is easy to do under saddle once the horse has learned it in hand.

Moving sideways over poles is not a natural movement for the horse. Here again, he'll learn to coordinate new movements and to evaluate obstacles from a different perspective.

### Ground Pole Exercises

Asking your horse to negotiate poles placed in various patterns, at different distances and heights, you will be teaching him to lower his head and neck to look where he's going. He'll actually be mentally involved in what he's doing and will learn to estimate and control his movements, which most horses today don't have much opportunity to practice. Confined most of their time in the stall, they have an impaired sense of dealing with their environment.

When a horse lowers his head to see where he's going (see figure 99), he is no longer in a position of flight. He's learning to use his eyes in a new way and to calculate what his four feet are doing. This activity of tracking the movements of each foot and learning to use each one individually again furthers his ability to learn.

Start with six poles spaced on the ground about four feet apart. Either round or hexagonal poles can be used as long as the poles are to be used on the ground. For most exercises in which the poles are raised it's best to use hexagonal poles as they don't roll so easily.

Lead your horse up to the poles at a walk. Before you come to the first one, halt, lean down a bit, and tug gently on the chain until your horse mimics your bent position by lowering his head and neck slightly. Then lead him in this posture across the poles. If your horse is very nervous, you may have to walk him across a few times before he'll keep his head relaxed. Until he does, however, you cannot consider this exercise successfully accomplished. To make it absolutely clear to your horse that you want him to stretch down, you can offer him a bit of feed in a shallow container or from your hand (see figure 150).

Once your horse is walking through the poles without difficulty, change the distance between them. Keep experimenting until the poles fit your horse's stride and he can walk through them easily. This distance will, of course, vary from horse to horse. Then change the distance again to keep him alert and to teach him to use his legs individually.

Next, space the poles one trotting stride (usually about four to four and a half feet) apart and ask your horse to trot over them, keeping his nose parallel to your shoulder and maintaining a distance of three to six feet between you (figure 83).

**Fig. 83**

Some horses are startled at first by the sight of the person next to them bounding over the poles. It won't take long, however, before they've grown accustomed to this as well. Each lesson that is easy and precise in its requirements lays the groundwork for a further, more diffi-cult lesson that will seem increasingly simple to master. Once your horse is trotting over the poles easily and with a regular rhythm, you are ready to increase the difficulty of the exercise.

You're now going to ask your horse to follow behind you over the poles, an excellent exercise to accustom him to following you over diffi-cult terrain, narrow paths and the like, without stepping on your heels or running all over you. If he gets too close to you, keep him back a bit by wagging the wand in front of him.

Next, place alternate ends of the poles up on a bale of straw or small barrel (figure 84) and again ask your horse to walk through (figure 85). This might be a difficult exercise for your horse, but keep your upper body bent slightly forward and he will usually trust you and follow along. If that doesn't work, go back to something simpler. Lift up only every second pole, leaving the others on the ground. The distance between the poles at the walk should be about two and a half to three feet.

Fig. 84

Fig. 85

Once the horse can walk through without difficulty, you can change the distance or the tempo, or put one pole much higher and the next two flat on the ground, or put two poles together on a single bale. All this requires the horse to think about what he's doing. The various heights and distances are also working the muscles of his back. As soon as one pattern has been mastered, move on to another one. Switch back and forth between wide and short-strided distances. Follow a flat pole with one raised to about one and a half feet. Each step he takes he'll be required to regulate his movements differently. He'll have to be even more careful where he puts his hind feet than he was in the labyrinth. Again, he won't just be able to let his hind feet follow the front feet as the pole which he's now negotiating with his hind legs might be quite high, while, at the same time, his front feet are making a flat, long stride.

If you find your horse getting tense, try putting the ends of all the poles up on one side and down on the other. Go through this pattern once from both ends. This will give both sides of his back equal exercise. After about ten minutes you'll find his back will be more supple and swinging. You'll then be able to increase the level of difficulty.

Once your horse has learned to move freely and independently through the various patterns, he'll be able to follow you or move alongside you on a long lead however the poles have been laid out, both at the walk and the trot (figure 86).

Be sure to repeat these exercises from the right side; it will not only improve your horse's coordination, but yours as well.

Your horse is influenced a lot more by your own movements than you may think. Horses tend to imitate, to mirror us. It's therefore quite important to maintain enough distance between you and your horse to

Fig. 86

allow him room to watch you move. If he's stumbling over the poles, pick up your own feet extra high. You'll be surprised how his performance will improve.

### The Star

Lay the ends of four to six poles on a bale of straw, a small barrel, or something of similar height. Then fan the other ends of the poles out on the ground about two feet apart to form the "star."

This obstacle will reinforce the lesson of the ground poles, teaching your horse to lower his head and neck, to look where he's going, and to keep his body relaxed in the bend required by the star. Find the path that approximates the length of your horse's stride. For a short-strided horse, you work closer to the center of the star; for a long-strided horse, work closer to the periphery. You can (and should) then vary the position from which you lead him, walking either on the outside or the inside of him, closer to the center or closer to the edge. The closer to the center you work, the higher your horse will have to step. Further out, he'll need to increase his stride. The star offers many possibilities for improving your horse's gymnastic abilities.

If your horse has difficulty initially with the height of the star, lower its center by placing the poles on something less high, a tire for instance. You can then increase its height gradually. If the tightness of the bend causes a problem at first, stretch the star out by laying the poles along another pole suspended between two barrels or straw bales (figure 87).

Fig. 87

It is important that you arrange your poles in such a way that your horse can complete the exercise each time with a feeling of success. This increases his willingness to try something a bit more difficult the next time. The perception that man and beast can only learn "by the sweat of their brow" is both obsolete and scientifically unsound as it ignores the principles that govern the functioning of the brain and nervous system. The more successful the learning process itself is, the greater the interest of the pupil will be, and the easier it will become to build on this base.

The star is a particularly good exercise to do under saddle. Go into a half seat and shift your weight slightly to the inside. Stretch your upper body forward and let your horse stretch down as far as he likes, allowing him to negotiate the poles totally unimpeded, alert, and with a swinging, relaxed back (figure 88).

**Fig. 88**

### The Grid

Another obstacle that can be used to instill confidence and coordination in your horse is the grid. The grid teaches a horse to place each individual foot carefully. This demands alertness and will give him greater conscious control of his movements.

The grid can be arranged in various patterns. Again, begin with the simplest and slowly increase the level of difficulty. In this lesson your horse will have to lower his head and walk through slowly and carefully.

This goes against his natural instinct to go faster when he's unsure of his situation.

In this exercise it's best to use hexagonal poles that won't roll if touched by a hoof. Place two poles on the ground parallel to one another and about six feet apart. Lay four other poles across these two, leaving a distance between them of about one and a half feet. Lead your horse through this grid carefully. Pick up your own feet and exaggerate the height of your steps. This will encourage your horse to imitate your movements. Stand about three feet in front of him to give him enough room to watch your movements and to get a feel of how best to imitate you.

Go slowly. It you push your horse too fast or punish him for making mistakes, he might try to rush through whenever he accidently touches a pole. When you approach the grid, stop and lower your own upper body when your horse is about three feet away from the first pole. Let him think through the situation a little, then proceed through the poles. Once he goes through the grid without hesitation, halt half way through so that he is straddling a pole. This increases the level of difficulty as he'll have to think carefully how to move his hind legs when he moves forward again. He's learning here to make conscious movements and to coordinate them. Once he can negotiate this configuration on the ground

Fig. 89

easily, you can increase the level of difficulty by placing the poles higher or, as shown in figure 89, by increasing their height from front to back. Adding more poles adds another degree of difficulty.

Whatever you do, it's important not to frighten your horse by putting the poles too high or designing too complicated a pattern. Nor is it a good idea to nail the poles in place. Do not overface your horse. Asking him to do more than he is ready for will cause him to lose confidence in you and in himself.

### Barrels

You can develop an entire training program around eight barrels. Line them up in two parallel lines, four on each side, leaving a narrow corridor through which you can lead your horse. This will teach him to tolerate the occasional object that might touch his side. Next, space the barrels somewhat apart and lead him slalom-fashion through them. This improves his overall suppleness, increasingly so the closer together the barrels are placed. Next, build curves (figure 90) and let your horse

Fig. 90

move both forward and backward through them.

It's frightening to the horse to be asked to go through so narrow a passage. Quiet him by letting him explore the obstacles with his nose

**Fig. 91**

until he relaxes and breathes normally. It will take a great deal of self-control for your horse to halt in the curve of a narrow channel and stand waiting for a signal from you to carefully move forward again. Any horse who's been schooled through the previous T.E.A.M. exercises knows he's not allowed to bolt through the passage. You can use the wand, your hand, and your voice to help him to "bend" if he gets stuck (figure 91). Whenever this happens with your horse, push his head in the opposite direction of where you want to direct his hindquarters. In the photo we're turning this mare's head to the left in order to get her to swing her quarters to the right.

To calm a horse's apprehensions, you might strew a little feed on the top of the barrels and let him eat. Don't be too forceful in your attempts to get your horse through the barrels. Banging around on them is not going to calm his fears. As with other obstacles, he'll learn that the barrels are not a danger to him only if you proceed quietly and with patience.

### Ground Driving

You'll need two lightweight ropes or lines that can be attached to the lower rings of your horse's halter and then run through the stirrups as shown in figure 124. The stirrups should be adjusted to about the length of the skirt of the saddle. Were you to attach the lines to a bit, the horse would tend to come behind the bit (tuck in his nose too much). The mere weight of the lines causes more pressure than we want on his mouth and acts to bring the horse behind the bit. Any stress would then cause him to become overcollected and tense. This would counter our objective here, which is to get him to relax his back and stretch. Driving with a halter facilitates this goal. The saddle accustoms the horse to carrying weight. Running the lines through the stirrups will make your signals to turn clearer because the stirrups will move a little off to the side as your shorten the lines to turn.

Driving from the ground has many advantages, particularly with a young horse. The horse can learn to stop, execute turns, and wait for your signals to move without having to deal with the added and confusing weight of the rider (or the rider's incorrect aids and reactions in some cases). In just a few days you'll develop a lot of self-confidence in your horse by teaching him these signals from the ground. Begin by having an assistant at his head with the customary chain and wand.

There are many other advantages. The feel of the long lines against your horse's body and around his haunches gives him a new sense of his own body. This is particularly important for nervous, tense horses—the kind of horse whose owner tells us can't be driven from the ground because, "he shies at anything that touches his sides or legs." This kind of horse especially profits from ground driving. The light touch of the lines gives him a growing, more conscious perception of the parameters of his body. It might sound strange that this is necessary, but consciousness of one's body and self-confidence are closely related. The more areas of his body your horse can feel in a new way, the more self-confidence he'll gain.

When a horse has been taught to drive from the ground and has learned to relax while being worked, he will also know under saddle that it's best to keep calm when he gets into trouble. If, for example, he were to get caught up in some fencing wire or get a branch caught between his legs, a green horse would panic. Driving teaches a horse to overcome his response of fear to such a situation.

It's also quite useful to drive the horse through various obstacles and on short hacks to get him accustomed to other new situations. If you have a difficult horse and feel unsure about going out in a halter, use a bridle. It would be better, however, to take along a knowledgeable assistant.

*

## TEACHING YOUR HORSE TO OVERCOME FEAR

### *"The Terrifying Plastic Sheet"*

For these exercises, you'll need a thick sheet of clear or white plastic about four feet wide by twelve feet long. These exercises, in which you'll ask your horse to walk over and under plastic sheets, are, along with the labyrinth and poles on the ground, the best cure for a nervous horse who tends to shy. Our modern environment is ridden with plastic that flaps and crackles in the wind. If you can get your horse used to the various forms, shapes, and sounds of plastic, he will learn to trust your judgment, overcome his fear, and later defer to you in other terrifying situations.

Working with the plastic sheets—walking your horse over and under plastic—and the ability this develops in him to override his fear has such a lasting effect on the horse that we can actually talk of a change having taken place in his psyche. Just think about it—he's an animal of flight. Once he's learned he can control this flight reflex, he'll accept almost anything.

**Teaching Your Horse to Walk Over Plastic.** We start with something easy. Lay out the plastic sheet and weight it with a couple of rocks so the wind doesn't move it. Lead your horse as close to the plastic as he will willingly go. If he's afraid and props his legs, snorts, and refuses to move further, stop where you are in the exercise and quiet him (see figure 133). Fold the sheet into a small, long strip about one foot wide. Bring the horse closer and halt again. Don't ask for anything else at this point; don't even try to move his head to get him to look at the "monster" more closely. After a minute or two of standing quietly patting and talking to your.horse, give him a treat, then step over the plastic strip and halt.

Usually the horse will pick up his courage and follow you—often making a tremendous leap to the other side. For this reason, be sure to give him plenty of room to the side and hold the lead quite slack.

Next, sprinkle some grain on the plastic, ask your horse to lower his head, and let him eat. Asking the horse to move with his head and neck stretched low is important for all T.E.A.M. exercises, but absolutely necessary for the work with the plastic sheet. Horses convince themselves that a given thing is harmless by sniffing and touching it with their noses. A nervous, unsure horse will try instead to flee whatever seems dangerous. First he throws his head up, signaling alarm and stimulating his entire nervous system in preparation for flight. You'll need to show him you want him to stretch down by bending your own upper body forward and giving soft tugs on the chain to put gentle pressure on his nose (figure 92). Make sure not to pull, as this could result in his pulling back

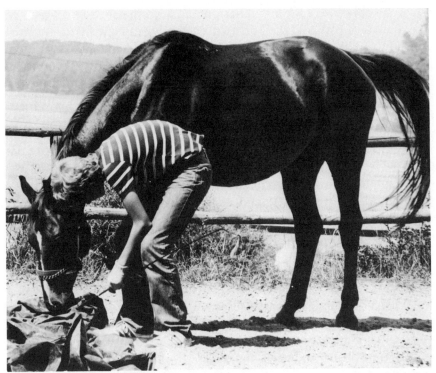

Fig. 92

Fig. 93

—just the opposite of what you're trying to accomplish. Some horses respond better if you hold the horse's nose gently with one hand and press carefully on his poll, massaging the spot behind his ears with your fingers, or if you move his head softly back and forth. By lowering his head, the horse relaxes his back, hips, and poll. It changes the urge to follow the flight reflex *and* brings him further along toward submissiveness to man without force. With his head lowered he automatically feels more secure and protected.

As your horse's courage grows, touch him on the croup with your wand and give a little pull on the chain to ask him to come forward. Once he quietly crosses the folded plastic, spread it a bit larger, sprinkle more grain on it (figure 93), and start the exercise anew until he finally walks calmly over its entire width. It sometimes helps to have a second horse who is quiet and already knows the plastic to show your horse it's safe to walk on. At this point you don't want to pick up the plastic or cause it to make any noise that might frighten him.

**Teaching Your Horse to Walk Under Plastic.** For this exercise you'll need two jump standards about six feet tall or something of similar height. Lay a strip of plastic across these so that the plastic doesn't hang down too low (figures 94 and 136).

Nervous horses and ones who tend to back up under saddle or shy to avoid going past something scary will profit the most from this exercise. Your horse will learn to use his eyes in a totally new and unaccustomed way. He'll learn to deal with an absolutely unnatural situation and to control his fear. He will learn to obey and trust your signals no matter how nervous he might be. Every experience should teach him, "Wow, that looked really scary—but it wasn't anything after all!"

Place a bucket of feed on the ground in front of and then under the plastic bridge. The feed provides your horse with an incentive to stay put, even when his instincts are telling him to flee. A horse who's eating will also find it impossible to hold his breath. He has to breathe freely and this induces relaxation. Of course, it can take a while before he'll actually stick his head under this terrifying obstacle to get at the bucket (figure 94). As your horse gets comfortable eating from the bucket, move it further away from him so he'll have to move under the plastic to eat. We'll be describing this exercise more when we relate Rex's case (see page 137).

Walking under plastic is another exercise that helps the horse develop self-assurance and teaches him to act sensibly in new or frightening situations. As long as such exercises are practiced without stress or force, they help develop a horse who watches what we do with ever-renewed interest and trust.

**Fig. 94**

The correct use of the chain and wand continues to be very important in these exercises. Simply getting a horse to follow us over or under a piece of plastic any which way wouldn't profit us much at all. It would merely reinforce the horse's old way to thinking—to get out of scary situations as quickly as possible. This wouldn't be teaching him to think his way through the situation, or to trust and obey our signals.

### The Bridge
A bridge is "built" by placing a thick board, about four by eight feet, flat on the ground. When your horse walks quietly over this, raise the platform four to eight inches on blocks or poles and try it again. Many horses are frightened by the hollow sound of their steps on the bridge, as well as by having to step up onto the bridge and down again. Once they've gotten over their fear, they'll not mind the hollow tone of stepping on a trailer ramp either. Exercises with the bridge are particularly helpful with horses who don't load well.

### The Seesaw

The seesaw builds on the bridge exercises. As with the bridge, the wooden plank is placed flat on the ground. With a very nervous horse, you can make a railing on either side of the plank with two jump poles raised on eight-inch blocks. When your horse walks onto the board, halt him in the middle, offer him a treat, and let him stand there for a few seconds before leading him off. Once he does this easily, lay a small log under the middle of the board to create a little seesaw effect. Lead your horse to the middle, let him find his balance, then lead him forward again. The height of the seesaw can be increased gradually to about sixteen inches. You can vary the exercise by asking your horse to back down again after he's reached the middle. When your horse is moving quietly over the seesaw, you can dispense with the side rails. In the beginning, most horses will feel ill at ease with this movement under their feet, but you'll also find others who really enjoy seesawing.

Horses who are used to the bridge and the seesaw and taught to follow under the plastic sheet with the tap of the wand shouldn't be any trouble to load in a trailer.

### Branches

Prune a few long twigs and small branches from bushes and trees. Cut some with leaves, others without. Lay these in a rectangle on the ground and let the horse walk across them with his head lowered. You might want to confine the branches with a few poles to keep them from being scattered.

This is another exercise designed to increase a horse's self-confidence. It also makes him safer to ride as he won't panic on hacks if a branch gets caught between his legs or stuck in his tail.

Horses who spend their entire lives in a stall, far from any natural existence, often fear branches and logs on the ground. For the very fearful horse, start by creating a small corridor, about two feet wide, through the branches. Have your horse follow you through the corridor on a long lead, then halt in the middle and stand there a while. This will also prepare your horse for circumstances where he needs to follow you down a narrow path without stepping all over you. Each time you walk your horse down the corridor, bring a few branches in closer until he's stepping over them. Again, halt in the middle, give him a treat, and then walk on.

Endurance and event horses are going to profit especially from these lessons as they will often have to forge through new territory—over fallen logs, bushes, and thick undergrowth. T.E.A.M. horses soon learn to pick their way with care through difficult, uneven, muddy areas to find the safest path. Once a horse has learned to "think" for himself and evaluate a terrain, an experienced rider will usually leave it up to the horse to find the best way through a rough area.

Note: We've not included an illustration of this exercise because we felt it didn't need a detailed technical description. Nevertheless, we believe it to be a most important lesson. No training program would be complete without it.

### Automobile Tires

Teaching a horse to stand with one foot in a tire is actually a very practical exercise. Nearly every horse owner will one day need to soak and cool a horse's hot, injured, swollen foot. The easiest way to do this is, of course, to place the foot in a bucket, but most horses who aren't used to this knock the bucket over in no time. Once you've trained your horse to stand quietly in an automobile tire, you'll have no future problems asking him to stand with his foot in a bucket.

Walking through a row of tires is another exercise that exposes the horse to nonhabitual movements and increases his awareness of his body, which develops his innate ability to learn.

It will take time and patience for you to get your horse to step into a tire. This will be easier to teach if you create a corridor to and from a tire with two poles (figure 95). Your horse will find it more natural to follow this path. Take him up to the tire, stop, and using your body language and light pulls and releases on the chain, ask him to lower his head and

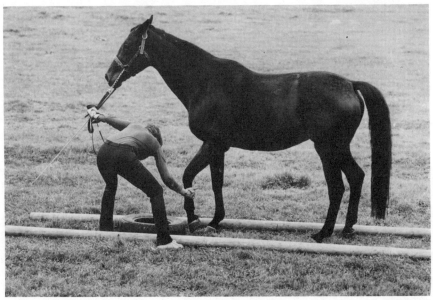

**Fig. 95**

neck to explore the tire.

Once your horse has lowered his head, lift one of his feet and place it down in the tire (figures 95 and 96). When his foot is in the tire, lead him forward. Keep a light contact with the chain so that he doesn't step back again. You want him to step over the tire with his second front foot and step into it again with one hind foot (figure 97). If his hind foot doesn't land in the tire this first time, that's not too important. That will come in time. Repeat this process five or six times, praising him each time he steps through the tire.

It is up to you whether you want to give your horse a treat each time you praise him. Just make sure he doesn't get so distracted looking for treats that he starts begging and poking through your pockets when he's supposed to be concentrating on his work. A friendly pat on the neck will usually suffice for praise, but there are no rigid rules on how best to reward a horse.

Some horses get so dexterous in their work with tires that you'll soon be able to devise various patterns with several tires and have them walk through. Other horses, however, seem to find this exercise particularly difficult.

In the course of our long experience with horses, we have found the following tip helpful in teaching the tire obstacle. Lay as many tires down next to one another as possible, creating a surface totally composed of tires. Create a path through this tire surface with poles set on barrels or hay bales. The horse will understand that he has to get through this mess somehow and will look for a passable way. When he

Fig. 96

Fig. 97

tries and steps on the edge of a tire it will flip up and bang him in the knee. Nevertheless, after all the previous exercises, he'll know that these round, black "monsters" are basically harmless (see the exercise with branches). Keep reducing the size of the tire bed until, as in the beginning, you're left with a single tire between the two poles, and, as you've wanted him to do from the start, he should now walk through it.

A more advanced variation of this exercise is to have the horse stand with one or both front or hind feet in a single tire following these procedures and those used to teach a horse how to stand (see pages 52–56). Not only will he gain more confidence in himself, but another of our original goals —that he stand quietly in a bucket to soak—will have been achieved.

## WORK WITHOUT A HALTER

One of the biggest rewards of your intensive and detailed work with the halter, wand, and chain is that you will have gained so much control and developed such a trusting relationship with your horse that you'll soon be able to go through all the exercises without the restraint of chain or halter. To start with most horses, simply remove the halter. You should still use the wand as an extension of your arm to signal him to keep his distance by holding it in front of his nose or tapping his chest with its butt end. If later he doesn't listen to your command to halt when you're working without the wand, you can place your hand on his nose

**Fig. 98**

and press into its cartilage with your fingertips.

If you don't feel quite secure enough to do the exercises completely without tack, tie a piece of baling twine around your horse's neck (figure 98). The disadvantage to this is that you can come to rely on it too much and wind up just pulling your horse behind you. At this point what you're aiming at is to control your horse's every movement, asking him to stop, walk on, and lead, *just* with your voice and body language.

Don't use your body to press into your horse's shoulder with your elbow or to grab him by the nose and lean back into his chest to stop him. Try to get a response with the least amount of effort possible so that

**Fig. 99**

the horse learns to respond to your subtlest signals. Later, under saddle, he will also follow the softest squeeze of rein or leg. You want this to become second nature to him.

In more advanced work, in the labyrinth, for example, there will be times when you'll have to place your hand lightly on your horse's nose or hold your hand under his throat to help steer him. Or you might have to ask for a turn on the forehand with one hand on his nose and the other tapping softly with the wand on his quarters. These exercises are actually more difficult for the person than the horse, as it will take a whole new kind of coordination for you to be able to use your hand this lightly without bumping into your horse with your elbow or shoulder. You will have to be in balance. At the same time, you'll be standing closer to your horse and using your body language alone to ask him, for example, to bend down to take a closer look at something (figure 99).

It won't be long before your horse will follow you freely around the school or pasture (figure 100). This is an especially satisfying experience with horses that were previously nervous and fearful.

After your horse has mastered these exercises you won't need to

Fig. 100

halter or tie him for grooming anymore either. Figures 101 through 103 illustrate our goals and methods in tackless grooming. This intelligent Arabian is standing quietly to be groomed. He registers every movement. He no longer fears the wand as an instrument of punishment as he has long since learned to accept it as an extension of the human arm (figure 101).

Fig. 101

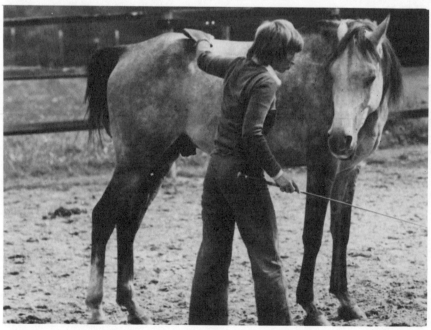

Fig. 102

Because his back hurts, he resents being groomed even with a soft rubber glove and relates his resentment to the groom by turning his head and pinning his ears back. This is his means of communication—his only language (figure 102). In response, his handler touches him with the wand lightly under his chin to prevent him from moving off to the left (figure 103). Should he try to move forward, she'd hold her hand and the wand in front of his face and tap gently with its tip against his chest. His ears relax as he now knows from experience that she has understood and will groom more gently.

Tackless grooming can be practiced first in a stall or small paddock.

**Fig. 103**

## THE STATUE

This final exercise teaches patience and total obedience. Your horse is going to learn to stand like a statue—perfectly quiet and without restraint. He will continue to stand still when you walk off to get something, work on another horse, groom him, set up obstacles, or anything else. In figure 104 we see the lead hanging to the ground. With practice you won't need halter or lead at all. When tacked, your horse will stand still with the reins lying on his neck.

To train your horse to do this exercise, start by standing him in his halter and chain shank. Back slowly away from him until you've reached the end of the lead. If he's understood and learned his previous lessons, he'll know he's not supposed to move until you signal to him with your voice, the chain, or a tap with the wand. When he's standing still, move a little to the right, then a little to the left, and then return to his head. Keep your arm stretched out toward him and maintain a distance from him of at least four and a half feet. If you move too fast or breathe unevenly or quickly, your horse won't stand still. If you really concentrate, though, it will have an almost hypnotic effect on him.

Should your horse misunderstand what you want and follow you—even just a tiny step forward—move him back to exactly the same spot he was standing at before using the backing techniques on pages 81–83. Soon you'll be able to get him to move back to his original spot just by

Fig. 104

holding the wand in front of his nose or tapping his chest with its handle. By this time you should be able to drop or remove the lead shank.

You should soon be able to reduce all this to a quiet command, "Stand." This needs to be said at just the right time—specifically, just as you feel your horse is about to move.

Horses learn the meanings of various gestures and words as well as dogs do. We just don't usually give the horse a chance to demonstrate this. Of course, whatever signal you give for your horse to stand is going to work better the quicker you can react to his first inclination to move. If you aren't concentrating and alert, you are not going to be able to react quickly enough and will have to start the exercise over again and again. Give the command, "Stand!" exactly at the moment when you perceive him begin to lift his front foot. He should promptly put his foot back down again.

Once your horse has learned to stand like a statue, you can turn from him to talk with other people or do whatever else you like; however, it's important that you keep him in sight, if only out of the corner of your eye.

The statue is bound to impress other horse owners, but like all the other T.E.A.M. exercises, it has a far more important effect. Anyone who works through these exercises with his horse is going to understand that success is attainable only with the greatest patience and thought. Such a trainer will also be incapable of brutality or harshness in the saddle. The carefulness developed during the in-hand training will carry over to the horse's training under saddle. The riders relationship to his horse under saddle thus also will become one of trust and gentleness.

# Six Case Studies: Work in Hand and Under Saddle

Six case studies of horses of different breeds and sizes who came to us with a variety of problems will serve to demonstrate how the application of the Touch and use of the structured T.E.A.M. exercises can turn "rogue," stubborn, resistant, unsound, hypersensitive, and nervous horses —horses lacking in their mental and physical balance—into quiet, relaxed, cooperative partners with whom it is a pleasure to work.

*

We want to emphasize again at this point, however, that the Telling-ton-Jones Method could be seen as the elementary phase in the training of *all* horses. Every horse—young, green, or well-trained—can be schooled in this way, profitting both the horse and his owner greatly.

The understanding and routine established here can then be applied over and over again in a horse's more advanced training under saddle. This will be especially useful if your horse begins to resist new and more difficult training requirements. The exercises will help you to nip such resistance in the bud. Both horse and rider will soon recognize how much more pleasant riding can be when both are working together as a well-coordinated team.

## Introduction

For the sake of clarity, we'll use the same format to describe the six case horses and the procedures we used to correct their problems. We'll begin by describing the horse's personality and physiological characteristics. Then we'll explain the application of the Touch, what we focused on in the work in hand, then our experience with the horse under saddle, and, finally, the success we achieved.

Because the described methods ran concurrently, you will need to integrate these mentally by working through each case study in your imagination. Were we to lay out this work in precise detail each case study would provide enough material for an entire book.

## KAISHAN

We'll first go back to our original case study, Kaishan. Please review the description of his problems from Chapter 2. The nature of his main problems, namely:

1. pain in his back and neck,
2. lack of manners, and
3. total lack of contact with people

dictated the focus and direction of our work with him, specifically:

1. use of the Tellington Touch to relieve the pain;
2. use of in-hand exercises to teach him to relax his body and to be well-mannered and obedient; and
3. use of strategies to help him develop a cooperative relationship with people.

Methods 1 and 3 ran concurrently. In our first attempts to teach him to stand quietly, we encountered that expressly disinterested, almost disgusted look of his with which he dismissed all efforts to communicate with him. In response to the wand signals to stand, he would turn his head to the side or half close his eyes. We just couldn't induce him to look at his trainer. If we gently turned his head to the front, he'd roll his eyes away as if to say, "You can do what you want, I'm still going to look where I choose."

His stallionlike instincts told him to dominate—mares, possible rivals, and people. It took almost two weeks to get him to stand without constantly screaming to "his" mare. More than any other horse in this group, he needed to be handled and touched a lot on his head and face.

He needed to be stroked. He needed to be introduced to a friendly touch, taught to accept it, and finally brought to appreciate it.

We worked patiently with him for hours on end. The Touch brought him quick relief from the pain he felt in his neck and back. Soon he let us touch his face, even without being held. Exercises bending his neck back and forth were very important (see figures 17–19) in controlling his automatic reflex to throw his head up from the moment the rider mounted. The hand is so important in working with the neck. It works much better than any mechanical device could to hold a horse's head down because it spreads warmth, moves with his head, relaxes, and re-assures. The trainer would bring Kaishan's head around to the side, prac-tically wrapping his neck around her own body. This was also an impor-tant means to establishing contact. This exercise is called "Yielding the Head." Once a horse will give to the pressure of the hand, he'll let his neck relax under saddle as well. When he stretches his neck down, his back will be able to swing and carry the weight of the rider. Being mounted and ridden won't cause him pain any more.

Above all, Kaishan loved the *Chua K'a*, or skin rolling (see pages 27–28). In the beginning, his handler steadied Kaishan's head with one hand while she began to gently roll his skin with the other. Soon she was able to use both hands to implement the technique, which was, of course, more effective (figure 105). This work is best done without a halter, as a degree of trust can be established and deepened in this way that cannot be attained under the restraint of a halter.

Fig. 105                                   Fig. 106

Kaishan's posture in figure 106 clearly shows how very much he's enjoying his "massage." His head is low, he's totally relaxed, and he's chewing softly, moving his lower jaw back and forth. You can tell that your "massage" is having the right effect if your horse stands with his eyes half closed, moving his mouth, licking his lips, and swallowing.

After a few days' work, Linda took Kaishan out under saddle to see if he was as impossible as his owner had described, or if, perhaps, his owner was just a little inexperienced or inconsistent in her aids. We tacked him as usual, using a snaffle bridle and an all-purpose, German-made saddle. He threw his head up immediately and jigged around, his head twisted to the left. If another horse in the group got too close, Kaishan would try to wheel around and threaten the "intruder" with stallionlike trumpeting. He also tried to get Linda into trouble several times by brushing his right shoulder into a fence or a tree.

Linda then rode him back to the barn and exchanged his usual saddle for a Western one that had been specially designed to fit Arabians. This kind of saddle spreads the weight of the rider over a larger area of the horse's back and ribs. It kept the back muscles that Kaishan would automatically stiffen from coming into contact with the saddle at all. At first, there was little change in his behavior (see figure 1).

The change came when Linda substituted a roller bit with shanks and double reins for his accustomed snaffle (figure 107). It ended up that Kaishan actually had quite a soft mouth when he wasn't throwing himself into the bit to run away from the pain in his back. This new bridle, with a double rein attached to a curb bit with long, loose, curved shanks and a copper roller for Kaishan's tongue to play with made quite a difference in getting Kaishan to relax. Within just a few days, she was able to control him without his becoming tense. She used some of the Touch techniques behind his ears while she rode him. Since he'd learned to relax his neck in response to this treatment on the ground, he did it now under saddle almost as a matter of course. He began to stretch down, which automatically relieved much of the pain he'd caused himself by throwing his head up and depressing his back.

We were ready to try him again in a group. Linda worked him first in a large mowed field using exercises designed to accustom him to the control of the rider and teach him to behave better in the company of other horses. During this time, the other riders worked their horses about 170 feet away. Kaishan, in the meanwhile, was getting used to this new way of being ridden—without pain. The special bit encouraged him to round his neck, keeping the muscles on its underside soft. The Touch techniques made him feel quite obviously relaxed and he stretched his neck down in a way that a chambon, for example, could never have forced.

Fig. 107

After Linda had worked Kaishan for about ten minutes, the other riders began riding closer and passing them. Linda continued to work to soften Kaishan's neck. She praised him for his behavior, which made him feel good as the other horses moved closer.

Following this first attempt, the work with him was continued in the smaller arena—primarily in hand.

To teach Kaishan patience, we left him standing tied for about one hour each day in a place where he could nibble hay and watch other horses at work. We next moved to working him in hand in a small arena in which other horses were being ridden. He soon learned that he wasn't allowed to act aggressively towards the others. He was then brought into the arena in a halter and lead chain. The first time another horse approached, Kaishan obeyed his old reflexes and lunged out, screaming wildly; in short, acting the unruly stallion.

Linda smacked him with the butt end of the whip on his nose, telling him in a low but brusk voice to "Whoa!" It was necessary to use a rather hard rap to get his attention away from the others and to prevent his pulling against the chain as he had previously pulled against the bit under saddle. The smack gave him quite a shock and stopped him immediately. He backed away instead of rushing forward as he usually did. From this point on, we had his attention. As soon as he began to scream, he got another rap on the nose. It didn't take him long to understand,

and from then on the handler was the boss. Soon his handler was able to stop him with just a gentle tap, a sign that she had won his respect. It was a small step from this to Kaishan's acceptance of and reaction to our subtlest of signals.

*

In dealing with a difficult horse, it's easy to make the mistake of being too gentle—or too harsh. People who aren't very self-assured themselves believe that if they are simply kind to their horse, the horse will return this kindness. If the horse has learned to respect people, this might well be the case; but the horse must first have learned that people are higher in the pecking order. With T.E.A.M. work respect can be gained without abusive treatment.

This requires that you see each horse as an individual and treat him accordingly. A fearful, insecure horse (see Dutch, page 122) will have to be treated with more patience. A stubborn one (see Mini, page 160) will require a lot of consistency and resolve until you're accepted as the boss, an absolute prerequisite to working together with your horse as a partner.

A horse is going to obey if your signals to him are clear. This is why it is so important that you stand up by his head when you do the ground exercises. This enables him to see clearly every gesture of your hand, your shoulder, and the wand. Perceiving your body signals, he'll know to stop without your even having to pull and release on the chain.

*

Prior to every lesson under saddle, we first worked with Kaishan in hand, using Touch techniques and exercises through an ever-varying course of obstacles designed to teach him to look where he was going. He found walking over the plastic sheets interesting (figure 108). Though he's half shut his sensitive eyes to the sun, his ears are forward, his neck is relaxed, and his head is held low. His handler has bent her own body forward and is using this body language to encourage Kaishan to do the same.

The most important ground exercise for Kaishan was work over poles, which required him to stretch down his neck and open his eyes to see where he was going, using his back in a nonhabitual way. This brought him relief from his pain. He wasn't afraid of the poles on the ground as is often the case at first with Arabians. Thus we were able from the beginning to alternate their heights, giving his back maximal opportunity to move as Kaishan walked over the poles from both direc-

Fig. 108                    Fig. 109

tions. This had a different effect than it would have had under saddle. We continued to vary the pattern of the poles so that he would have to watch and pay careful attention to where he was going— and so that he'd have to halt and decide how he was to put down each foot. All these exercises were designed to develop in him the habit of thinking about what he was going.

Soon he was following his handler over the poles without a halter. Like many Arabians, Kaishan was particularly intelligent. He seemed to be telling us, "This isn't so bad; it might even be more interesting than lounging around the paddock all day." The handler remained one step in front of him during this work to allow Kaishan to see her own move- ments and to encourage him to imitate her. A horse whose trainer is stiff and awkward in negotiating the poles may also be stiff and awkward. If your horse stumbles a lot at first in these exercises, you'll find it will help immensely if you demonstrate what he is supposed to do by exaggerat- ing your own steps. Try it. It will also help if you tap the hoof or leg that he keeps bumping into the poles with your wand. This will make him more aware of this particular leg.

Kaishan had refused all the first week to stand quietly tied. He had needed to be supervised the entire time and corrected gently. Following that initial sharp rap on the nose, however, he finally seemed to have understood what we wanted. After that it was no problem to teach him the statue (figure 110). Here, his trainer is leaning somewhat towards him with her weight on the balls of her feet. She's giving him her full

Fig. 110

attention, controlling him with her voice. The whip is simply a reminder to stand. Soon, she was able to turn her back to him completely or walk around him—while all the while the other horses he had been so aggressive towards were being worked close by.

We next started working Kaishan in the arena under saddle, expanding on the lessons of our first excursion. We rode him in pairs, continually changing partners, and practiced passing and letting others pass. We had him negotiate obstacles that required a lot of concentration both alone and next to other horses. He soon began to enjoy the challenge of something new and interesting. His lively spirit and quick mind, which up to this point had been focused exclusively on thwarting people, discovered more pleasant, varied, and painless occupations. Throughout this training we continued our treatment of his back and neck with the Touch techniques aimed at getting him to stretch his neck and round his back.

Prior to our next group hack, we led Kaishan for walks in the countryside (figure 111) so that he would learn to relax outside, to stretch down even further, and to swing his back. We wanted him to be able to enjoy these excursions. He loved nosing the ground and exploring exactly where to place his feet. All this had been impossible before. His former owners had kept him in a stall and ridden him in a martingale. He had always been too fired up to be ridden on a looser contact, which would have allowed him to explore more.

After ten days of work in hand and under saddle in the arena and short hacks outside where he was led along with other horses, we took

Fig. 111

Kaishan out on a group hack. He made one attempt to bite the horse next to him, but a rap with the butt end of the whip reminded him of his manners and peace was reestablished. Thanks to the exercises in the arena, he now permitted other horses to follow closely behind (figure 112). His back no longer hurt and he was able to hold his head in a more comfortable position.

Fig. 112

Part of our overall success came from frequently changing Kaishan's riders. The riders in this program were all amateurs still learning to ride. They were instructed to reward him by massaging his neck and to assure him they were interested in him by talking with him. Each new rider took the time to get to know him. In this way Kaishan's trust was developed in all riders, not merely in a single person.

At the end of three weeks of our training Kaishan, his two owners were able to ride him out on a loose rein without any difficulty.

A year later, Kaishan returned to Reken to take part in a ten-day gymkhana course. He recognized the place immediately and was an enthusiastic participant. You could do anything with him, even, as you can see in figure 113, ride him in just a halter.

**Fig. 113**

*

A large contributor to Kaishan's success was the bit we used. His first owner had ridden him in a snaffle and martingale, driving him strongly into the bit. Because Kaishan had learned to pick up his head to escape, the martingale had been necessary to get him under any kind of control at all. Of course, this just made his ewe neck worse. Bitting him with something easier on his mouth and neck solved his problems quickly. Working with a normal snaffle would have taken a very experienced rider at least six months of consistent retraining to get him to relax. In the end, too, Kaishan probably would have reverted to his old habits as soon as he was again being ridden by his owner.

Using the T.E.A.M. training bit,* Kaishan felt better in days. His neck became rounder and longer. This took the pressure off the poll, which always develops when a horse is driven too harshly into the bit. Our training bit (figure 114) might look harsh, but it has been designed carefully to ensure the comfort of the horse. (There are other bits which look similar but which don't have the same effect. One is purposely designed with fixed shanks to shorten the stride of the horse.)

**Fig. 114**

The T.E.A.M. bit has rings for a second, upper pair of reins, which makes it most suitable for horses who pull or rush. A normal curb isn't appropriate to use on a high-strung horse because it will make the horse more tense. The use of the top rein of the T.E.A.M. training bit quiets the horse and prevents him from tucking behind the bit. The lower curb rein rounds the neck and acts as the "brakes." This bit should be used with an English cavesson to prevent the horse from opening his mouth and escaping from the action of the bit. The reins are normally held so that contact with both reins, not just with the upper or lower pair, can be maintained.

If your horse doesn't stop at your signal, check the fit of the curb chain. In measuring the fit, you really can't in this case rely on the rule of thumb of two to three fingers' space between the chain and the horses chin, because fit is also determined by the shape of the horse's jaw. It's better to try to get an angle of about 45 degrees between the shank and the horse's mouth when light contact is established with the lower rein. This method is similar to that used when measuring a Pelham or double bridle. If the horse continues to rush, it is usually an indication either that the chain is too loose or the bit is lying too low in the horse's mouth.

---

*This equipment can be ordered from T.E.A.M. headquarters. Ordering information can be found on the back page of this book.

Countless horses have difficulties with riders who use the snaffle in-effectively. Isn't it better to help a horse who has become a puller or a shyer or who has otherwise become totally unresponsive to the snaffle by using a bit that has proven itself effective in making both the rider and horse happier? Why stick to using a snaffle at any price when things could be so much easier?

We suggest a rider inexperienced with the use of two reins ride with reins of the same length. We recommend ½-inch and 3/8-inch reins, with the upper pair a bit wider than the lower pair. In this way, no matter how you hold the reins, you'll know which is which and will soon get used to them.

## DUTCH

Dutch is an eight-year-old Dutch-bred warmblood gelding of un-known bloodlines. He towers at seventeen hands.

### *Personality*

We can see from his head (figures 115 and 116) that although Dutch is a nice horse, he's not very intelligent. He'll need a long time to learn

Fig. 115

Fig. 116

anything. His sleepy eyes set high on his long, narrow head; his long, active ears; and his most unusual profile comprise a rather strange portrait. At first glance, he seems to be Roman nosed, yet the little indentation in the middle of his nose and the change in the line of his forehead from convex to concave point to a horse who can be recklessly brave at times and very timid at others. He was, indeed, this mercurial under saddle as well, but generally he tended to be more timid and hesitating than he was bold. He has worry lines above his eyes. These and the triangular indentations above his eyes point to insecurity and fearfulness. The shape of his cheekbone denotes a certain inflexibility, and the angular drop towards his nostrils reveals a streak of stubbornness. His very loose, pliant upper lip indicates a readiness to accept people; he trusts people as a matter of course. This is a horse who has a hard time doing what's asked of him both because he is in pain (as we learned later) and because he's slow to understand what is being asked. But he's also a good-hearted horse who continues to try.

### Exploration of the Body

Our first exploration of Dutch's body brought dramatic results. Figure 117 indicates the areas where he showed pain to even the lightest touch. He wouldn't allow us to touch the area between the first and

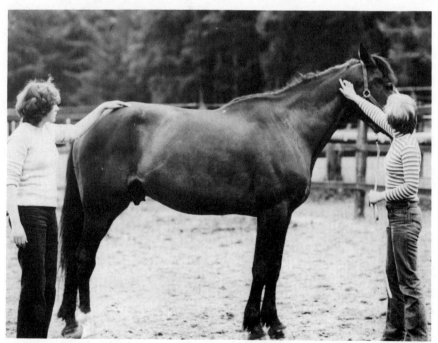

**Fig. 117**

second vertebrae of his neck at all, and he threw his head up immediately in response to our approach. It's possible that he had once badly injured himself here. His entire back was sensitive. He tolerated being
brushed on his back, but cringed visibly in response to the pressure of
our fingers just behind his withers. He seemed most sensitive of all in the
pelvic area and at his hip joints. Pressure of our cupped fingers here was
enough to make him falter and then stand balancing that leg (figure 118)
on the edge of his hind hoof, his whole back held cramped with pain.

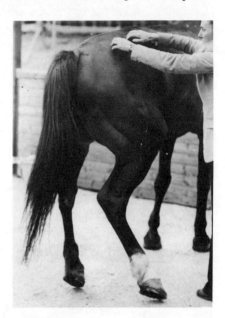

**Fig. 118**

### Conformation

His sloping shoulder and long pasterns endowed Dutch with a wonderfully long trot. This was something of a problem in that he had never
learned to control the unbelievable forward energy he produced. His stiff
back tended to increase this forward imbalance. His impulsion was
glorious to watch, but not easy to sit.

### Conclusions

Due to the pain in his hips, his basically timid character, and his inability to think well or learn quickly, Dutch was a real problem. He had
neither self-confidence nor self-control. His young owners had bought
him to be an endurance trail horse because of his unusually long, fast
trot, but they'd never been able to get all this energy under control.
Under saddle, Dutch would begin to pace and then would run away. Our
examination of his body showed why. The pain in his hips and back

made him stiffen his entire body against the rider's weight. This caused him to pace (see figure 122). Then the pain became so bad that he would panic and simply try to flee.

### The Touch Technique

Dutch, our most difficult horse as it turned out, needed long, patient work on his body. We started on his neck (figure 119), gently probing and "massaging" until he enjoyed that so much that he'd drop his head ever lower in response to the gentlest touch of our fingers behind his ears (figure 120). We would press in, then relax the pressure, feeling into his neck. This gentle kneading felt wonderfully good to Dutch. His every reaction showed that the Touch was getting through to him.

Fig. 119

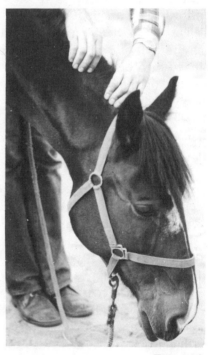

Fig. 120

It must be kept in mind that all use of the Tellington Touch is done without force. You can't really *force* a seventeen-hand horse to lower his head. Even an amateur, however, can learn the subtleties of this 1 to 10 touch (see page 28). Dutch's owner came to our school several times a week with his wife to practice the technique. You see him in the photographs working the painful areas of Dutch's neck with his fingers. By doing this he is "massaging" away the discomfort Dutch feels in his painful neck vertebrae. Secondly, he is teaching Dutch to lower his neck in response to the Touch, which will further relax the tension in the irritated area.

Dutch achieves this relaxation by using his muscles in a nonhabitual way. At first it was necessary to press one hand down on his forehead or to tug a little on the chain while the other hand continued to work behind his ears until this big, ungainly horse noticed that this Touch felt good and freed him of pain.

The second neck vertebra in Dutch's neck protruded to one side more than the other, and every time we manipulated his head from left to right the vertebra popped out with a crack. We used *Chua K'a* (see figures 24–26), gently rolling and pressing the skin to improve the circulation in his back, which would lighten his hindquarters. This also helps the horse gain confidence in the hand and to accept its touch over his entire body without fear, just as later he'll learn to accept the rider's weight in the saddle. After just two days of our working intensively on Dutch's body for fifteen minutes and giving him easy exercises to get him to turn his head (see figures 17–19), Dutch would let himself be touched on the back and we could push down on his croup without him totally caving in.

This horse had been bought out from under the noses of the meat men by his idealistic owners—without doubt a good deed. As problem mounted on problem, however, they named him "Sheitan," which means "devil." How were we going to make a good mount out of a horse who'd been given a name like that out of sheer frustration, and then had been treated as if he were indeed a devil? The first thing we did was to rechristen this horse "Dutch" because of his breeding and because it was a short, cheerful, friendly name. For similar reasons, we also renamed Mini and Dali (see pages 160 and 172).

### T.E.A.M. Ground Exercises

When we began working with Dutch in hand, it was immediately obvious that he was afraid of everything new to him. We worked first on getting a quiet walk and trot in hand and then on getting him to halt without our having to tug on the chain. The walk was no problem; the trot was another story. Due to Dutch's tremendous forward energy in the trot, his handler was constantly pulling on him to keep him slow. Our goal was to have the horse slow down of his own accord and stay next to the handler instead of mindlessly rushing off. Dutch had no sense of balance whatsoever, which in turn made him even more insecure. Again and again he tried to catch his balance by running forward. This just put him more and more onto his painful forehand. We spent the next few days asking him simply to move one step forward and one step back, teaching him to shift his weight back onto his quarters. This was the first step towards better balance and self-confidence.

*

The horse is a being of motion. His entire security rests on his ability to move lightly and in harmony with a mental as well as a physical balance. When this balance, normally taken for granted, is lost, whether from fear, pain, or the fact that the horse, having spent his life in a twelve-by-twelve stall, is no longer capable of correctly coordinating his legs, an inner fear grows. This fear results in shying and flight.

Even an amateur can help a horse with poor balance once this has been identified as the cause of his problems and the horse knows that his problem is understood. In Dutch's case, we used the ground exercises to help him find his balance, to slow him down, and to help him override the instinct to flee.

*

It took much longer and demanded much greater patience than with the other horses in the group to get Dutch to walk on the plastic sheets. It took days for him to understand that the plastic was not a monster ready to swallow him up. Each obstacle he was able to negotiate, though, made it somewhat easier for him to learn the next one.

He was terrified of the wand and would run if it were merely lifted while he was being longed. We recognized that not enough work had been done at the beginning to get him used to it. It hadn't been used enough to stroke all parts of his body. Neglecting the basics of acclimating the horse to the wand happens often because

1. the handler feels the horse knows all this already and won't get upset by the wand;
2. the handler feels his whip-shy horse will never get used to it, so why upset the horse or himself; or
3. the handler feels during the initial sessions that the horse is getting too upset and quits, thinking it too risky to continue.

Somewhere along in the training process, however, such omissions become costly. In our case it took days before we were able to start Dutch longeing again on the short line. We went back to stroking him a lot with the wand under his belly. He jumped away a few times, but then accepted its touch. At this time, Dutch walked quietly and stood well, but the moment something frightened him, or if he were asked to turn too sharply or abruptly, he would jump into a trot and storm off. During this time, his handlers became experts at using the wand to give very light signals for him to move forward or to back up. They still had a little difficulty with the chain, however. To use the chain correctly, you need to have a lot of either innate or learned sensitivity to its use.

Dutch's handlers continued to work him in hand two hours a day. Once, asked to walk through a zig-zag corridor through the barrels, he panicked and tried to rush out (figure 121). By this time his handler had learned to stretch out her arm instead of trying to hold him back with

**Fig. 121**

her elbow. It would have been better still if she'd held the butt end of the wand in front of his face. We brought out a bucket of grain and gently stroked his body with the wand again to get Dutch used to things touching him. Still, it took days before he really got used to it again. He'd get used to having the wand touch one part of his body, but would run off as soon as we touched him somewhere else. He'd gotten used to the wand up front and under his belly, but when we tried to approach him from the rear, he lost all self-control and we pretty much had to start from scratch again.

All this work was of immense importance because it is much easier to teach a horse to control his panic from the ground than it is later under saddle. You're able to reinforce this control with the chain, and the horse doesn't have to contend with the extra weight of the rider, pain in his back, or pulling on his mouth. Thus, we avoid the vicious circle: pressure on his mouth causing tension in the neck and subsequent pressure on his back; that pain causing him to run away; his running away causing the rider to put more pressure on his mouth.

When Dutch was finally able to get through the zig-zag course successfully, without tensing his neck or holding his breath, we knew he was on his way to being able to accept new lessons without regressing into old patterns of behavior.

### Under Saddle

Linda had to call on all the skill and experience she had accumulated in her thirty years of training horses to keep Dutch from panicking and taking off the first time she rode him in the arena. We had put both a Lindell* side-pull hackamore and a short-shanked Arabian curb bit on him (see page 157). A horse with a very painful back and hips can not be balanced from his mouth, so we tried to influence him with pressure on his nose instead. The combination of the Lindell and the curb prevented him from running away and kept him from carrying his nose too high. He already had a saddle custom-made to fit his high withers. Linda rode him carefully, pushing (not driving) him only slightly into contact with the Lindell and curb. Nevertheless, it was very clear after ten minutes that the horse was in stress and pain.

It was impossible to get Dutch to do a proper walk; he paced clumsily and was ready at any moment to take off (figure 122). Linda could not give him a longer rein so that he could stretch his neck. Just at a walk, his breathing rate skyrocketed from its normal 20 breaths per minute to 120. It didn't make any sense to continue riding Dutch until he had lost his fear and overcome his instinct to run away from everything. We also realized we'd have to continue to manipulate his neck as we've described to get rid of the stiffness and tension in his neck and body. He didn't need training in manners, though. In contrast to Kaishan, Dutch was obedient and very much a gentleman.

Due to Dutch's extraordinary learning disabilities, it took two full weeks before we were ready to ride him again. And, again, due to his fear and tension, he was so inflexible that he literally fell out of balance, which increased his anxiety.

We then changed to the roller bit and a Western saddle. Because Dutch had high withers, it wasn't easy to find the right saddle, but with enough padding we finally got an acceptable fit. In the roller (see figure 114), his mouth got softer and he became more flexible at the poll. Within

---

*The Lindell can be ordered from T.E.A.M. headquarters. Ordering information can be found on the back page of this book.

**Fig. 122**

two weeks of the tack change he was working on the very lightest contact.

Linda worked Dutch a lot in the "half step," which is a slightly collected walk. The horse moved forward—step by slow step—only half as far as with a normal step. He wasn't being pushed in to the bit any more, which further helped him find his balance. Riding him in simple curved lines just six feet in from the long side of the arena was enough to throw him off balance. To help him find it again, Linda would halt and let him stand for about thirty seconds.

One might wonder why we trained a horse selected for endurance trail riding in an arena. We've found, no matter what the horse is going to be used for, that the combination of the Tellington Touch, T.E.A.M. work in hand, and thoughtful riding in the arena will help a nervous horse find his balance and self-confidence most quickly. It won't help to ride him on trails if he's going to resist your aids the entire time (nor will it do much good to drill dressage figures with him in the arena all the time). Dutch would have just become more nervous, caused himself more pain, and become increasingly tense if we'd tried to hold him back outside, which would have been necessary to keep him from taking off.

Instead we rode him a lot over ground obstacles until he understood them. He then visibly enjoyed finding his own way through the labyrinth on a long rein, knowing to halt at the slightest signal, and waiting in balance for the signal to move on. We also used an exercise taken from Western riding—turns toward the wall—done quietly to help him further better his balance.

All the exercises were easy. For Dutch the most important were the exercises over cavalletti and obstacles constructed from poles. For example, we constructed one such obstacle by placing two poles about four and a half feet apart and laying another four poles horizontally across them about two and a half feet, or one stride, apart (they were about four inches off the ground). They were not fastened down, so they would roll if Dutch got going too fast and hit them with his hoofs.

A clear round required a lot of concentration on the part of both horse and rider. If Dutch rushed through the poles uncertainly, the rider got off and led him through a few times. If he still didn't quite trust the situation with the rider up, we put the halter and chain on under his bridle and had him led by a second person from the ground while the rider just sat quietly and took up a very light contact on the rein. This helps many horses who've had bad experiences with riders. (A "bad experience" usually means an experience wherein a horse has been unjustly punished when he hasn't quite understood a new lesson. As a result, he has learned to associate "new" with punishment.)

＊

It is of paramount importance that the style of riding suit the situation. For horses with painful backs, it is necessary for the rider to change from a full to a half seat. Sometimes this single change alone can bring about a monumental change in the horse's behavior.

＊

By the end of the fourth week, Dutch had moments when he was able to trot around the arena confident and in balance. He'd actually gotten to be a pretty horse; he blew softly through his nose and was attentive with his ears. His tail, always a sure barometer of his moods, swayed quietly in rhythm with the trot (see figure 123).

Unfortunately, these episodes never lasted very long.

### Ground Driving
Dutch just couldn't get rid of his fear of things coming up on him

**Fig. 123**

from behind. He'd get nervous and excited and, consequently, lose his balance—the same old story. This indicated that Dutch just wasn't that intelligent. A smart horse learns quickly when something new is patiently presented to him; a horse who's less flexible, both mentally and

**Fig. 124**

physically, needs a lot more time. Of course, even with a slow horse, it shouldn't take half a lifetime, just more effort and thought on the part of the handler and a carefully established working relationship with the horse. The one reward from working with this kind of horse is that once he's learned a given lesson, he's often learned it for good.

To cure this fear we ground-drove Dutch (figure 124). In the beginning he was afraid of the touch of the lines on his quarters. He got over this fear relatively quickly, however, as he had already learned to accept the touch of the wand there. The lines were attached to his halter, not to a bit, and, of course, not to the chain. Many people ground-drive using the bit, but we wanted Dutch to learn to move quietly and in a relaxed manner. Under saddle, pressure on the bit had caused him to tuck in his chin, lean forward, and go even faster. Without any pressure on his mouth, he now learned to move in a given tempo until a signal on his nose told him to slow down or halt.

We drove Dutch like this for hours—out on hacks and over every possible obstacle in the arena. This worked fairly well at the walk, but when we started work at the trot, we needed assistance again (figure 125). Because of his overly strong forward impulsion, Dutch had a hard time holding himself back. Other than the walk, he'd really only known one tempo—full speed ahead. The helper at the front holding the lead with the chain would use the wand in front of Dutch's nose to slow him down. We wanted Dutch to learn to control himself in the trot as well as in the walk. He needed to slow down in response to a signal until he understood how to balance himself and was able to trot in a regular rhythm on an even longer line. Of course, the goal was to have Dutch capable of doing all this under saddle as well, but a horse whose back is

Fig. 125

so painful and who's so totally out of balance will be more successful under saddle if he learns this self-control in hand first.

Getting used to the wand and ground driving were to be the two lessons which had the greatest and most lasting influence on Dutch.

### Change of Riders and Final, Lasting Success

After two weeks of being ridden by Linda, Dutch was much improved. His breathing rate at the walk sank from 120 breaths per minute down to 80. Of course, this was still too high, but it was clearly an improvement. As soon as we changed riders, however, he'd fall back into his old ways. With all the other horses in work, we'd change riders on a daily basis to make them more patient and improve their alertness. Most of them didn't mind at all, as all our riders were working on the same exercises and under our constant direction. The horses found the exercises interesting and the riders took time to establish a personal contact with each horse they rode. This didn't mean that we all rode to command in a group. Each rider was given specific exercises to work on based on the individual horse's level of training and ability to learn.

This changing of riders was difficult with Dutch. Due to his insecurity and previous bad experiences, for Dutch each new rider became a potential tormentor from whom he would run uncontrollably (figure 126). For every inch of progress we made, it seemed we'd have to move two inches back. It was obvious he wanted to learn, but it was equally frustrating that he learned so slowly. I'm sure a lot of people felt all this a waste of time, that "a few good whacks would teach him!" Perhaps once in a great while a totally ruined, thoroughly bull-headed horse will come along with whom such a method might work. A horse who's in pain like Dutch, who tries to understand, even though his instinct to flee overrides everything else, would probably graduate from that school of training to wind up just where Dutch's story started—at the door of the slaughterhouse.

Others might question whether it pays to invest all this attention in such a "worthless" horse. His owners had saved him from slaughter, had fed him, had had him correctively shod, had had a saddle custom-made for him—and had still wound up with a horse that any "real" rider would have laughed at. Why? Because they loved him. They saw him as a member of their family—not as some means of satisfying their ego. Even love, however, can wear thin under such pressure.

Dutch's owner was a good rider. During his frequent visits he and his wife learned how to use the various Touch techniques and the T.E.A.M. exercises important for Dutch. We kept Dutch in training an additional two weeks for free because we weren't sure that even our training was going to help such a slow learner. His owners then took him home and

**Fig. 126**

hitched him to a wagon. This was a rousing success. They were very pleased. When they began to ride him again months later, Dutch had become a new horse. He was self-confident, unafraid, and trusted "his" people. They then began to train him for competitive trail riding—and it worked from the start. Since then, Dutch has been a happy horse, winning over middle distances. He also has a very happy rider.

*

The photos in figures 127 and 128 were taken at a competition about one year after Dutch left us. With his rider in a half seat, Dutch is trotting free and long, his ears forward, and his tail quiet. Such pictures say more than words ever can.

Linda describes his head: "He looks proud. He knows he's a success and is enjoying his life. It also looks as if his intelligence has grown significantly. Although he still doesn't have a very fine head, it has definitely gotten more elegant. Just compare this picture with the ones taken in the beginning (figures 115 and 116). People had helped him get rid of his pain and his anxiety—now he's showing his gratitude with his health, dependability, and success."

**Fig. 127**

**Fig. 128**

# REX

Rex is a large, powerful seven-year-old Haflinger. His owners wrote of him, "The smallest scrap of paper on the path, a sign, or something that hasn't been there before frightens him. He then jumps way off to the side, turns around, and takes off at a gallop. Plastic bags and similar things that flap or rustle are a major problem. Once he takes off like this, he can only be stopped with a tremendous amount of force. He also doesn't like to be out front in a group."

His owners didn't have the strength to hold him back. Since they lived close to a large city, each time Rex ran away with them became an increasingly life-threatening situation.

## *Personality*

Rex has an interesting face (figure 129). The bulge between his eyes is often a sign of irrational temperament. However, under the bulge comes a little dip, which is rather abnormal, followed by a round nose known as a moose nose. The moose nose is always an indication of a very strong-willed character and is often found among herd leaders or horses high in the social order. Rex's short, pointed chin usually accompanies a tendency towards inflexibility. He's a slow learner who can react irrationally to unfamiliar circumstances. The rather blank expression in his somewhat chubby face also points to fairly low intelligence. On the other hand, his mustached lip tells us he's probably a horse who'll

**Fig. 129**

cooperate happily once he's understood that he can move freely without getting pulled on by his rider.

Viewed from the front (figure 130), Rex's eyes are set wide apart, which in cold-bloods is not always a sign of intelligence. If, for example, wide-set eyes are combined with the bulge described above, the latter is of greater significance in determining personality. His ears are far apart and of medium length. This points to a quiet temperament. He doesn't open his eyes completely. This could mean that he's nearsighted. His nostrils are not large, but are fully opened, an indication that he's interested in what's going on around him.

**Fig. 130**

Rex's normal way of standing (figure 131) with his head and neck held very high is particularly notable. From our experience, this often points to an eye problem—sometimes nearsightedness, sometimes a problem with depth perception. This might be the reason that Rex suddenly makes these huge leaps to the side while out on a hack. The muscle of his neck when he holds it up like this is abnormally tensed and his flight reflex is twice as strong. Such a posture is also uncomfortable for the horse, and he connects his feeling of discomfort with everything he fears. If he'd lower his head and neck and look, strange things wouldn't seem so frightening. He'd be able to see and smell them better.

**Fig. 131**

## The Touch Technique

Our goal was to get Rex to lower his head and neck, so we didn't work a lot with the rest of his body, but focused our daily work along his crest.

Aside from his unpleasant tendency to shy, Rex was an unproblematic, well-mannered horse. He was an easy keeper, easy to groom and tack, and usually mannerly under saddle as well. He was generally easy to control and halt either when being ridden alone or in a group. What he hadn't learned yet was self-control.

❋

We often speak of a horse's inborn flight reflex. It's exactly this reflex that Rex needed to learn to control. In our times such an instinct is not only useless to him, it's downright dangerous.

To override the flight reflex, we first needed to alter his stance, ever posed for flight. To do this, we did not use a martingale or other means of force, however. Instead, we taught him to halt correctly and to trust our judgment. If we were to tie his head down with a martingale, he'd still not stop were something to panic him, as horses ridden in martingales have proven time and time again. If anything, he'd just run all the more to free himself from its unpleasant constraint.

❋

Rex's problem was clearly defined. Of course, we could have fitted him with a roller bit and ridden him out on hacks. We'd have been able to halt him if necessary. However, this wouldn't have done anything to cure his readiness to shy, as indicated by the tense, high carriage of his head and neck, nor would it have increased his self-control.

### T.E.A.M. Ground Exercises

Thus, from the start, we concentrated on challenging Rex with difficult obstacles on the ground. If he had been a nervous or generally tense horse as Dutch had been, we'd have taken more time teaching him to lead and other simple exercises. As it was, we proceeded directly to working with the plastic sheets.

You can work the plastic sheets into the learning process in a number of ways to fit individual horses. One method that doesn't work, however, is beating the horse into crossing over a plastic sheet. This would be a totally negative influence on the horse, confirming his initial suspicions that there was something to fear about the plastic.

With a fearful horse, we usually fold the sheet together into a long narrow strip that he can easily step over (see figure 92). Once he will do this, we feed him from the plastic and gradually spread out one end until he's walking on it.

If a horse is truly panic stricken, you can place the plastic perpendicular to a wall, leaving enough space between the plastic and the wall so that he can walk between the two. Each time you lead him past, give him a little grain, holding it lower and lower until it lies on the plastic. Each time also have the plastic sheet brought closer to the wall until the horse eventually walks on it.

Many horses will lose their fear if they can stand next to the plastic and watch other horses walk across it. (This is true of all lessons.) It's important, though, to work quietly and to ensure that the other horses complete the exercise without difficulty. Many horses are upset by watching a horse being punished. (This is why it is inadvisable to let other horses watch attempts to load a horse who is difficult. Also, if another person loses his temper and resorts to force, yelling at or hitting his horse, get your own horse out of there. Such experiences can all too easily rob him of his trust.)

With Rex, we didn't have to be subtle. We started with the sheet spread out to its full length and width. As he was brought into the arena, however, a sudden breeze caught the sheet and caused it to move. Rex shied, tearing the lead out of his handler's hand and charging to the other end of the arena, completely terrified. If a horse has gotten out of control once, it can happen again if precautions aren't taken. For this reason the next time we led Rex to the plastic we first ran the chain through his mouth (figure 132) and gave it a short tug to get his atten-tion. This wasn't done harshly or in a punishing way. If we had punished him for running away it merely would have increased his fears.

If the chain is used through a horse's mouth, it is preferable if the rings of the halter are round, rather than square. The halter should be po-sitioned higher on his nose than normal, with the noseband lying a little less than two fingers' width under the horse's cheekbones. If the chain lies too low it can pinch the corners of his mouth against the halter rings.

**Fig. 132**

Passing the chain through Rex's mouth might sound harsh, but this enormously strong horse had gotten completely out of control. He had grown hysterical when confronted by this flapping object that he couldn't evaluate correctly because he held his head up so high.

As we led him back toward the plastic, his breathing increased to 88 breaths per minute while he was just standing still. (A normal respiration in this situation would be under 30 breaths per minute.) We led him around the arena a few times until he was concentrating more on the chain than on the plastic. When we led him again to the plastic he stood with his hind legs braced stiffly; his neck and ears seemed frozen (figure 133). At this point we offered him a handful of oats. As he lowered his head to eat and reached forward for the oats with his lips, his fear abated somewhat. We led him again and again up to the plastic with the lead slack, giving him an occasional short tug to get his attention. He tried once again to run away before he noticed that with the chain this was no

Fig. 133

Fig. 134

longer possible. When he relaxed again, he was immediately rewarded with oats and a friendly word. For the first time in his life he was standing his ground in the face of something frightening. Slowly it began to dawn on him that the people around him seemed to have the situation on the ground well in hand and that he could trust his safety to their keeping. After he'd been offered the grain bucket several times, it was set down on the plastic sheet—and he ate from it (figure 134).

A few minutes later we poured some of the grain directly onto the plastic sheet. The handler gave Rex time and a long line to give him the feeling that he could control his own next step. A tight lead would have only distracted and irritated him. The first time he touched the plastic sheet, he jumped away again (figure 135), but this time he didn't dash blindly off or pull away from his handler—he stayed under control. The handler gave him lots of slack. Anyone who is going to work with horses in threatening circumstances needs to be aware of the importance of keeping his distance from the horse under all circumstances so as not to be jumped on.

Within ten minutes, Rex was standing with his front feet on the plastic sheet. His head was lowered and he was concentrating fully on eating. When he moved forward a little, touching one of his hind feet on the plastic, he scared himself, jumped to the side, and looked back at his foot as if to say, "Hey—I made that noise myself!" His whole attitude changed and we were able to lead him back and forth across the plastic without any difficulty.

Fig. 135

For Rex, the plastic sheet had been an enormous confrontation. Once he'd learned to walk over plastic, everything else was relatively easy—going through water, crossing ditches, and loading in a trailer. Rex took all this in stride and seemed to think, "All this isn't bad at all—I'll eventually get something to eat and it's rather interesting as well."

His next lesson was in the labyrinth, where Rex was to learn to react to a short give and take on the chain, which, of course, had been taken out of his mouth and attached again over his nose in its normal manner. To get him to walk toward the handler, something new to Rex, the handler gave a slight tug on the chain and then *released again immediately*. This teaches the horse to really think about what he is doing, to wait for a signal, and, in time, to respond to ever more subtle signals. With a cautious, somewhat stubborn horse such as Rex, we wanted to activate a reaction and sensitize his nervous system to respond to various signals.

Work in the labyrinth makes a horse responsive to our least movement. In this way, parts of his brain are activated that, without these non-habitual movements, would lie fallow and unused.

Rex's third lesson was to walk *under* the plastic sheet. By the time he did this exercise, he'd gotten so much self-confidence that he didn't once try to run off as we led him up to it. Unlike Dutch, who seemed to take forever to understand and learn, Rex gained confidence and trust with every lesson.

Teaching a horse to walk under plastic takes patience to allow the horse enough time to think through what we're asking him to do (see pages 97–99). To review, here is the procedure once more. Take a minute to contemplate exactly what you want your horse to do, and then quietly lead him under the plastic sheet. Don't ask him to come forward if he's not yet ready to move. That encourages him to resist. It's best to wait another minute or two, then offer him a little something to eat. Let him eat, then ask him to come forward with a short pull and release on the chain. This is a signal he already knows. Of course, in the end, he shouldn't just know to follow the feed bucket—that's used in the beginning to get him to lower his head and to relax. Our ultimate goal is to have the horse follow us anywhere and for him to realize that he can feel quite safe in doing so.

After Rex had been led under the plastic sheet several days in a row —finally even without a halter (figure 136)—he was then ridden over and under the plastic in the T.E.A.M. roller bit. One day during this exercise, Rex's rider didn't bend down far enough and as a result pulled the plastic down with her head. Rex bolted, pulling the plastic behind him like a bridal train. Because he was wearing the roller bit, he was easy to stop. If he'd been wearing a snaffle, he'd have thrown his head up, tensed

Fig. 136

his neck, and would have been unstoppable. Instead his rider praised him for stopping, dismounted, fed him some oats from the bucket, led him again under the plastic, and then rode him under again without incident. He'd obviously developed enough trust to put up with such occasional mishaps.

Trotting over crossed poles (see figure 86) was another exercise we used to improve his coordination and to get him to use his neck more freely. At first he was a little afraid of the handler bounding along in front of him, but a friendly pat soon convinced him that this, too, was all right.

Rex particulary liked the later work we did, even without the feed bucket. Ears forward, he was obviously very content and pleased with himself as he went through all the various obstacles we'd laid out, even wearing a plastic coat over his back (see also figure 100).

Taking strolls is probably a most unusual mode of corrective training, but it gives a horse a large degree of confidence, not to mention enjoyment (figure 137). Rex stretched his head down and sniffed the ground like a dog. (It's such a sad sight to see a horse in a martingale and tightly buckled dropped noseband being ridden on a short rein through the woods. It's not much fun for the horse.) In the photograph Rex's handler holds the thick end of the wand about two feet in front of her

Fig. 137

Fig. 138

where she can easily and quickly bring it up in front of Rex's face if he should start to pull on the chain. A rap on the nose when necessary will make a lasting impression without making a horse head-shy. (She should actually be holding the lead rope a bit more loosely.)

Figure 138 shows Rex learning to stand still without restraint in the middle of a field where other horses are being worked. This taught him patience and again reinforced his self-control.

Everything we did in hand we were easily able to do with Rex under saddle. Figure 139, for example, shows his handler steering him carefully through the turns of the labyrinth. Rex has dropped his head to see better. His ears are alert. The fact that others around him are being worked, ridden, and jumped has long since ceased to distract him.

**Fig. 139**

Figure 140 shows Rex backing through the exercise. Because he'd gotten very relaxed, his owner wanted him ridden on just the lower rein of the roller bit, which offers a softer feel. Horses that have too much forward energy or who tend to get behind the bit should be ridden using both reins; but Rex didn't have these problems. It was more important with him, as with most horses who shy, that the roller prevented him from throwing his head up and taking off. Besides, at this stage he'd completely changed the way he carried his head and neck (compare figure 131) and could be stopped with the slightest squeeze. No longer was his behavior determined by his instinct to flee. On our rides out he never showed any inclination toward shying, running away, or displaying

Fig. 140

agressiveness towards other horses.

A year later his owner wrote to us, "Rex is a different horse. His fear has diminished so much that his reactions are completely normal. He rarely is frightened of anything, and when he is, he has learned not to run from whatever it is, but to take a closer look. This spring I even rode in a trail competition in which he was the only horse competing who was strange to the region. I'd never have dared to do this before. Of one hundred horses, he came in nineteenth. If someone hadn't removed one of the signposts, costing us twenty minutes, we'd have been fourth. Thank you for what you've done for Rex."

## HEIRA

Heira was a nine-year-old Icelandic pony mare of the best bloodlines. She'd grown up free in a herd and had been brought to Reken for the first time when she was five for her initial schooling. Though she'd never been mishandled, Heira had been so very shy of being touched at that time that all we'd been able to do was to make her a little less nervous around people. When she'd left we could saddle her and ride her a little. Throughout the next year, her owners reported, she'd remained difficult to catch and difficult to mount. The result was, as with so many dif-

Fig. 141          Fig. 142

ficult horses, that she had been ridden only seldom. Now, at age nine, she was overly nervous and so difficult to mount that it took several people to hold her. She moved sideways and tried to bite, rear, and buck. Once the rider was finally in the saddle Heira would jig and canter on the spot. She would throw her head up, pushing her lower neck muscles out. Her rider was given the distinct impression that he was sitting on a volcano. She didn't take off with her rider, however, and did both trot and tolt,* but in no time at all she would be covered in sweat.

### Personality

Heira's short broad head (figure 141) with fairly deeply set eyes is characteristic of a generally intelligent horse. Her ears are of average length, broad at the base and at the tips. This points to a steady, quiet personality. Her eyes are set well apart and her nostrils flair somewhat. These are all very positive signs. Her profile (figure 142), however, is rather complex as it blends several contradictory elements. Her forehead tends to bulge a bit over her eyes, then the line becomes somewhat concave and is followed by a moose nose. These characteristics are indicative of very different personality traits. The bulge above the eyes is often

---

*Translator's note: The tolt is a gait peculiar to Icelandic ponies. It is incredibly smooth and fast, similar to the rack of the American Saddlebred.

the sign of a difficult horse, the concave area points to timidity, and the moose nose shows strength of character. All of these traits were partially evident in Heira's personality. Her mouth is a bit short and her chin prominent. All in all this is evidence of a good—but complex—character.

### Exploration of the Body

Heira was first shown to us under full tack. Our exploration of her back under the saddle found it tensed and hard as iron. Obviously it was causing her pain. This is often the case when a horse's natural fear or incorrect saddling in the beginning causes him to tense his muscles in anticipation as soon as he feels the saddle on his back. The rather hard underside of the saddle then lies exactly on these tensed muscles, which run the length of the horse's spine. Soon this causes actual pain, which the horse tries to guard against by tensing his back even more. After a while this tensing becomes an automatic reflex that gets worse when the horse is being ridden because the saddle presses down even harder under the weight of the rider. To alleviate this problem we used a Western saddle on Heira, which distributed the weight of the rider more evenly.

Heira's chin was also like a rock and she was equally stiff in her neck (figure 143). With all these probings, she'd often hold her breath for long stretches. The muscles on the inside of her thighs were extremely tight

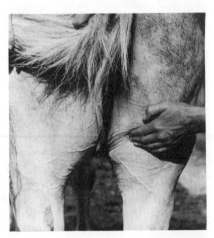

Fig. 144

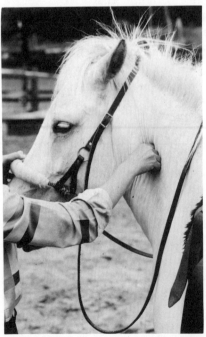

Fig. 143

(figure 144). Her owners had sent her to be bred five weeks earlier, but she had not conceived. Getting her to relax her thighs could lead to a successful future breeding.

### The Touch Technique

At first only Linda herself worked with Heira. When anyone approached Heira she would freeze and hold her breath. Her ears were noticeably pinned back and she looked mistrustful. Linda touched her gently; a lot of patience would be needed. In the first session, after thirty minutes, she suddenly shook her head as if something confining had just fallen off. Only ten minutes before, the skin on her back had remained totally flat and taut when Linda had pushed it together with her hands; now it could easily be moved (figure 145). Linda bent Heira's very stiff neck carefully around to the side (see figures 17–19), an exercise that proved later to be a key to her cure. Linda worked intensively with her ears (figure 146) to relax the hardness of her face that ran from her stiff chin to her stiff poll. Linda worked both the left and then the right side thoroughly.

The body work was of ultimate importance for Heira, and was used every day prior to the ground exercises. We focused on her head, neck, and ears. Heira relaxed visibly from day to day and would close her eyes in appreciation.

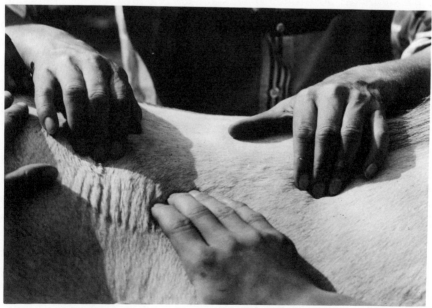

**Fig. 145**

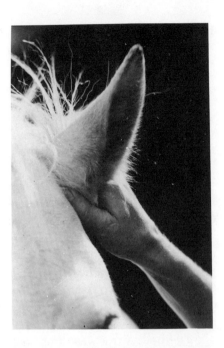

**Fig. 146**

At this point, I want to interject an observation that was verified by several of the alert people working with us at that time. The day after her first treatment, Heira stood sleepily in the paddock among the other horses in the sun. All at once she stretched her head forward and then to the left until her nose touched her shoulder. She then repeated the same stretch to the right, sighed deeply, and went back to dozing in the sun. She seemed to be repeating the bending procedure. It also seemed to be something new for her, an experience that had caused her to wonder and had felt so good that she was repeating it on her own. (We've observed hundreds of horses who repeat the stretching exercises with their legs (see figures 40–46) once they've had them done.)

### Saddling and Mounting

The first time Linda tried to mount Heira, she needed a lot of assistance. Heira immediately threw her head up, tensed herself as hard as a board, and had to be brought to a halt with much pressure on the Lindell (figure 147). Mounting was Heira's main problem, and that was where Linda began.

From this point on, we took our time. We didn't just quickly put the saddle on Heira and tighten the girth. Many helpers spent a great deal of time with her. They would place the saddle on her back and take it off again, then give her a treat. They gave her a lot of attention, patting and talking with her. Only when Heira relaxed and breathed did Linda proceed to the next step.

The next time Linda tried to mount her, Heira moved sideways and

**Fig. 147**

held her breath again. Instead of asking a helper to hold Heira, Linda took a small stool and simply sat down next to her (figure 148). She patted her gently and spoke softly to her without haste or pressure. There were deeply ingrained reflexes that needed to be overcome, something that wasn't going to happen overnight. Heira was going to have to think about what was going on and experience being mounted without fear. She had a habit of holding her breath and now needed to learn to exhale. Only when Heira let out her breath did Linda climb up on the stool, mount slowly, and dismount again. She praised Heira and gave her a treat.

Linda repeated the process from the other side (figure 149). As we've said several times before, due to the position of a horse's eyes on the side, he sees things new and differently from side to side. This is why it's so important to work with the horse equally from both sides. This is especially important if you're trying to overcome old reflexes and substitute new habits. An action on the left that triggers an old, bad reflex is

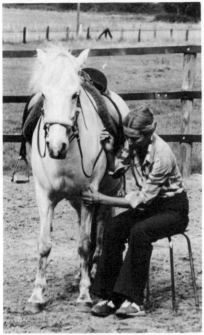

Fig. 148                                    Fig. 149

perceived as totally new when done from the right. When done carefully, mounting from the right is also safe. Little by little, this can be transferred more safely back to the left.

It's clear from the photo that Heira is *thinking* about what is going on. Instead of her ears being back, they are playing back and forth. Her poll is relaxed and her neck is rounded. All these signs indicate that she's given up her habitual tensing and is concentrating instead on what's happening. A horse must learn to think about what's going on.

Thus Heira learned step by step that being saddled and mounted wasn't going to hurt; that she didn't need to tense; and that it was much more pleasant to stand relaxed and wait for what comes next.

The stool had a double purpose here.

1. Standing on a stool or using a mounting block, the rider is able to mount without pulling the horse off balance.
2. Standing on the stool puts the rider at about the same height as the saddle. Thus a young, anxious, insecure horse can get used to seeing the rider positioned above him without anything else happening for the moment. Once the horse has gotten used to this, he's not going to be startled when the rider does finally sit in the saddle.

Fig. 150

Mounting from the ground was the next task. An assistant offered Heira a little feed as Linda slid lightly into the saddle (figure 150). (It's

Fig. 151                                    Fig. 152

best in a case like this to put the feed in a shallow tub so that a horse can get the grain without having to grab for a mouthful.) The feed fixed Heira in one spot and made it pleasant for her to stand still. The tub was held low enough to encourage her to keep her neck level and her back muscles relaxed so she could breathe normally.

This time while she was being mounted Heira was totally relaxed—in the photo you can see this in her tail, which hangs quietly. Heira's understood that being mounted is harmless.

As soon as Linda put her full weight into the saddle, however, the old reflex dominated again and Heira brought her head up, tensed her entire body, and held her breath again (figure 151). In the photograph she doesn't even seem aware of the presence of the feed tub lying on the stool next to her. Linda dismounted and showed Heira how to follow the feed tub down to the stool by lowering her head (figure 152).

Linda didn't hurry, and eventually Heira also learned to stretch her neck down with the rider in the saddle. This took time and patience, but not a lot of repetition. The steps in the learning process must flow smoothly into one another and must be designed to make the horse feel better with each learning step.

This method of teaching is an unusual way of handling horses. In the beginning, you may need a disproportionately large amount of time (we worked with Heira for three hours her first day). But subsequent lessons are learned very quickly and what is learned is also retained. (On the sec-

Fig. 153                                    Fig. 154

ond day, we worked with Heira for only an hour and then reduced our daily sessions to just twenty minutes. It wasn't long at all before she could be ridden on hacks.)

A new difficulty arose, however, when we tried turning her in towards the fence from the left. She wasn't able to bend her neck, but instead swung her entire body around all at once. We went back to a familiar exercise. Linda dismounted and gently turned Heira's head *down* and to the side. She gave Heira some grain from her hand (figure 153). Linda then drew her hand with the grain slowly back further toward the saddle. Heira watched and then followed with her head. Linda then used the same procedure on the right side. Heira was soon able to bend her neck much more easily. Linda next offered her grain from the saddle and Heira turned her head to take it (figure 154). Note in the photograph that she's turning down from the base of her neck now instead of from up behind her ears.

Linda dismounted again and repeated the exercise holding her hand slightly higher. Heira's willingness to listen to and follow Linda's directions increased quickly. Soon she was able to bend her neck softly in either direction and had no difficulty with the turn into the wall.

### T.E.A.M. Ground Exercises

Heira had no difficulty with the exercises in hand, so we were quickly able to work her through the obstacles under saddle. For this work she wore a Lindell—a bridle without a bit (figure 155). The Lindell works directly on the horse's nose without exerting any pressure on the

**Fig. 155**

Fig. 156

Fig. 157

nerves on either side of the head. The strap under the chin is made of soft leather and the nosepiece is made of stiff lariat rope. This bridle induces a horse to stretch his neck longer. Given Heira's fearfulness, she'd have been more nervous and tense with a bit in her mouth.

At first Heira had genuine difficulties bending her neck to negotiate the turns of the labyrinth under the weight of the rider (figure 156). Gentle pressure on the spot between the first and second vertebrae of her neck reminded her how. The labyrinth, when ridden at an expressly slow tempo and with frequent halts, both on the straightaway and in the turns, teaches a stiff horse to feel every bend in his body and makes him more flexible.

In the star (figure 157) it was especially important that Heira look carefully and appraise the situation before she began. Only when she participated with interest was she able to pick up each foot individually and place it carefully between the movable poles without causing them to roll. The rider can make this exercise more or less difficult, depending on how close to the center of the star he rides. Heira, stretching her neck low and breathing quietly, was soon able to pick her way through the star, no matter how it was ridden.

Linda summarized: "Learning usually refers to forming and changing a horse's behavior through helping him to acquire and refine his dexterity with specific movements. Heira's athletical ability was improved by using concrete and usual props, such as barrels, poles, plastic, and the labyrinth, with which she learned to work with and think with her rider. Work became more interesting and fun. All these exercises focused on making her more sure-footed and on stabilizing her mental and physical balance. The result was that she lost her fears that had been rooted in inflexibility and lack of balance. She relaxed and began to listen to what the rider wanted."

### Final Success

Heira got more and more flexible in mind and body. Soon she was accompanying the Thoroughbred Dali (see page 172) out on hacks (figure 158).

Her owner wrote us later: "I very much enjoy riding Heira now. After she returned to us it was clear that she was torn between her old and new experiences. At first she put on her old 'act' again, but I wasn't worried, as I could see she really wasn't taking it very seriously herself. We calmed her down with treats, by using the Touch along her crest, by talking with her a lot (to which she responded well), and with lots of patience. Today she's a model horse—we can catch her, tie her, and groom her without a problem. Her tolt is getting better by the day and she never tires. Even

Fig. 158

after I hadn't been able to ride for a while, she went so well despite the layoff that you could have thought she'd been ridden daily. It's clear that something learned thoroughly is something learned for life."

## MINI

Mini is a six-year-old purebred Arabian mare. She had grown up on a large breeding farm and up until just a few months ago was as green as a foal that had never been touched. Her owner wrote: "She was so good in the beginning. My sixteen-year-old son was already taking her out for hacks. Because she is so well bred and so very lovely I took her to be bred. When I went to pick her up a few days later, her nerves were shattered. She was nervous and tense. She was very fearful and wouldn't stand still at all. She couldn't be led without going wild, and any change in her environment made her shy dangerously. Water on the ground made her absolutely hysterical. She was unfriendly not only to people, but also to other horses, so much so that we couldn't turn her out any more. I didn't know what to do, so I registered her for the Problem Horse Course in Reken. I couldn't imagine that much could be done in so short a time, but what else was I to do?"

### Personality

Unfortunately, both photographs (figures 159 and 160) show Mini after she'd been with us for two weeks. They show her with a friendly, soft look in her eye. She has a flat forehead and a large, well-formed, relaxed chin. Her face shows average intelligence (for an Arabian). Her nostrils are narrow for an Arabian, indicating that she has not developed her ability to figure things out. Her ears are set wide apart at the base and are also wide apart at their tips, a sign of stable character. She is a follower, not a leader. Her long, fine nose and slightly dished face shows

**Fig. 159**                    **Fig. 160**

sensitivity and some timidity. Her chin is narrow, soft, and plump, but is capable of being drawn stubbornly together if she wants to get her own way (figure 161). This was typical of her reactions to all forms of treatment in her first few days with us. With her nostrils drawn back, her mouth clamped (a sure sign of dislike), and her eyes hard, she rejected our appeals for her cooperation.

Fig. 161

### *Exploration of the Body*

Mini was well built. She had a lovely head and a well-set neck. She had a good back; strong, straight legs; and hoofs that were healthy to the core, if somewhat neglected. We couldn't see her conformation being the source of her problems.

Nevertheless, Mini wouldn't allow herself to be touched anywhere without making her displeasure *very* clear. She'd pin her ears back ag-

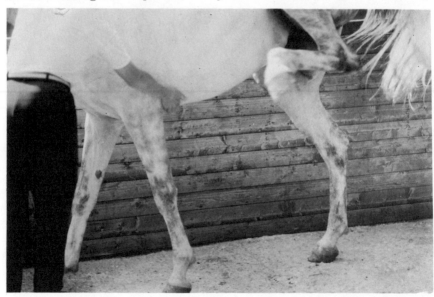

Fig. 162

gressively (see figure 163), often biting and kicking. If we touched her on her chest, she'd snap. When touched on the girth area, she'd kick out or cow-kick (figure 162). When the farrier tried to pick up a hind foot, she'd simply lose her balance and fall—which was why her hoofs were such a disaster. She didn't seem to be in pain. Actually, she seemed to be extraordinarily ticklish. This is a sign of hypersensitivity that results from muscle tension. With this kind of tension building in her body it was little wonder that she jumped yards to the side when she shied under saddle. That she didn't much like being touched was a trait she shared with many Arabians. She was also constantly in heat. Her owner didn't know if this had also been the case in the short time she had had Mini before taking her to be bred.

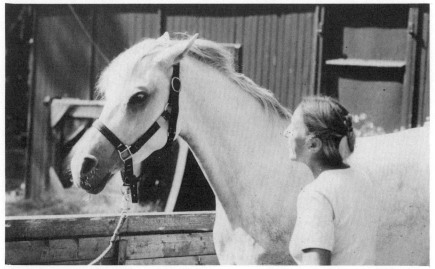

**Fig. 163**

### Conclusions

Mini obviously had a rather high opinion of herself. She also had no respect whatsoever for her owner and, as a consequence, wasn't at all interested in establishing a close relationship with her. Her tendency to shy dangerously was due to tension, lack of self-control, and the fact that she was never given a chance to learn during her first experience under saddle. She was now a coquettish young lady, too intelligent for most people's likes, impatient, and spoiled, who would allow no one to touch her.

### The Touch Technique

The foremost prerequisite for training any horse is that he allow himself to be touched anywhere—at the girth, on the ears, on the mouth, on the sheath or udder. Only when a horse accepts this can you feel confident that he'll not be a problem when working with vets or the farrier. This was the lesson we needed to teach Mini first, and it needed to be taught with lots of patience and a gentle hand.

When Mini was brought in for her first lesson she was impatient and nervous. She paid no attention to her handler and had no manners whatsoever. She was so uncontrolled that we didn't dare tie her to anything for fear she'd pull back on the rope, so we just looped the lead rope several times around a post. When we undid the lead rope to tie Mini somewhere more secure, she tried to take off and nearly ran Linda over in the process. Immediately Linda whacked her in the chest with the end of the thick lead rope as hard as she could. If she'd had the wand, she'd have given her a solid rap on the nose with its butt end. When it is necessary to hit a horse, as it was here, it's imperative that the trainer act quickly so that misdeed and punishment are unmistakably connected in the mind of the horse, and the effect of the punishment is immediate. In this case, it was important to get control of Mini's head again to stop her from taking off.

For the first time, Mini had found someone who wouldn't put up with her silly, ill-mannered behavior. (Her name was really Miruwi, much too arrogant a name for a horse with such a high opinion of herself, so we called her Mini, feeling this diminutive would bring her down a peg.) She stood still now, but wanted absolutely nothing to do with the people around her. Her laid-back ears and sour expression in figure 163 make it easy to guess what she's thinking.

We now began to work on her body. After about twenty minutes of gentle stroking and the soft probing, rolling, and thumping, Mini began to enjoy the touching. Her face that could mirror her every mood exactly —her flattened ears, the resistance in her eye, her nostrils that flared or drew together, her lower lip that almost curled—this face began to relax. Our first attempt to touch her hind leg, however, was met with a kick. Linda slapped her loud and hard under the belly. By this time Mini had learned that being touched wasn't going to hurt; she now learned that it was high time she stopped overreacting merely from habit. Immediately she allowed herself to be touched again, even at the girth and belly.

*

Mini was a valuable Arabian mare, which gave the value of our efforts a second dimension beyond mere correction. Mares that are as ticklish as she was often have problems with their first foals (or all their foals, for that matter). They don't allow the foals to drink because of their own hypersensitivity in the area of their udder. The owner often has to twitch a mare to distract her. The mare then connects this unpleasant memory with the nursing foal, which might make her feel less motherly towards him. It always pays to get a mare used to being touched on her udder by touching her there regularly when she's being groomed. It goes without saying that you need to be patient.

*

A few days later (figure 164): We've found a spot that Mini likes having scratched—we've won her friendship! Mini's whole appearance has changed dramatically. Her neck is stretched down and forward, her neck turned comfortably to one side. She purses her lips in pleasure. Mini has finally found out that people can be of interest for horses and can mean something good. (She'd already learned to stand there free without a halter.)

She enjoyed all the other head and body exercises with no complaints and various degrees of pleasure.

Not all exercises have the same importance for all horses, but the exercises on the head and neck should never be left out. Mini was soon able to bend her head easily to the left and right. This was another non-habitual movement that taught her to accept and comply with the handler's wishes and improved her balance (figure 165). She then began to ask for more contact. In figure 166 with her neck stretched down and eyes half closed she's enjoying the soft stroking and probing of the hands

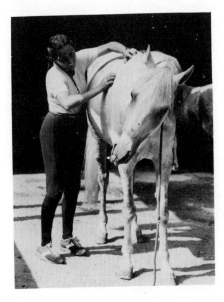

Fig. 164

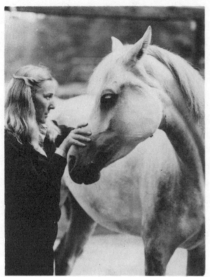
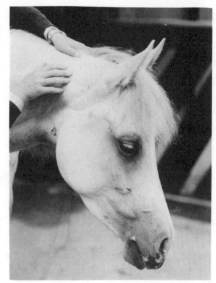

Fig. 165                                        Fig. 166

that has such an inexplicably calming effect on horses. Her impatience is gone, as is her lack of self-confidence and disrespect towards people. This is a new horse—one who has learned to listen, to respond to touch. She's learned through minimum but precise punishments and through patient understanding on the part of her trainer.

### T.E.A.M. Ground Exercises

The ground work ran concurrently with our Touch work on Mini's body, as usual. Mini progressed through all the lessons well once she'd gotten her abundant energy under control and had accepted the concept of standing still.

For the first several days we left her alone in the arena for two to three hours in the afternoon. At first she just went wild—she ran up and down the fence line nervously and without pause, moving her lower lip and rolling her eyes; however, she never once tried to jump the fence to get to where the other horses were (as she had done at home several times). We noticed that the longer she was out there, the quieter she eventually got. She learned right away that nobody was paying any attention to her commotion. But even when she stopped running, she'd flap her lower lip for a long time in an insuppressible physical restlessness.

One very thoughtful handler who was particularly interested in Mini took an inordinate amount of time teaching her to stand still. He sat down on a barrel in front of her and allowed her to move her head but not her legs.

She didn't want to stand still at all the first day and completely ignored the handler. Thereupon he gave her a hefty smack with the wand across her chest. (She was the only horse who had to be hit several times.) She jumped back, but became very attentive. He held the wand in front of her nose then, establishing a point that she wasn't allowed to cross. From then on she paid attention—whether the handler was on the ground or in the saddle. This single lesson drew her attention away from herself. For the first time she turned her interest that had been directed only at other horses to people whom she began to perceive as possible partners.

The trainer had Mini stand there quite still. he could anticipate any move she was comtemplating before she could carry it out.

*

Teaching a horse to stand is easiest taught from the exercise of walking a few steps and stopping on command. It will be simplest for you to teach this lesson if you start in motion. Ask your horse to take one step and then halt, walk, and halt again. Then ask him to move two steps and halt, walk, and halt again. Continue taking as many as five steps and halting. The horse will soon understand and respond to subtle signals. Whatever it is we want him to do must be so easy that the horse can comply without any stress or strain. At this stage, then, it's important to be very careful not to ask too much. What's most important is the patience of the handler and that he has an exact idea what he really wants.

*

Mini got more and more quiet and sensible. Her trainer told us, "Her view of the world has changed completely in just five days. Work that seemed incomprehensible and forced to her before, now makes sense. One step forward, one step back, picking up each leg, putting it back down again, lifting her head higher, walking over poles and around barrels—she does everything she's taught and she likes doing it because she's able to do it. Her nervousness is simply disappearing. She's going to school, and she's passing with flying colors!"

Finally Mini was able to stand quietly, untied, in the middle of the arena where other horses were working (figure 167) and not move a muscle, even if her trainer left her there.

Her quick intelligence was really awakened when she was asked not merely to stand still, but to walk next to her trainer over ground obstacles. Figure 168 shows one trainer with both hands up in the air to show that she's not holding onto Mini at all while the mare picks her own way with interest through the maze.

Fig. 167

Fig. 168

### Work Under Saddle

Since Mini's biggest problem was her shying at everything when she was being hacked, we did all our under-saddle work outside from the very start. Again, let's hear what her trainer had to say: "We went out and she was rather nervous. I gave her as much rein as she wanted and

**Fig. 169**

she immediately stretched down and moved her nose about eight inches above the ground from one object to another. She'd learned to do this over the ground obstacles. She took her time taking an exact look at everything. After about 300 yards she began to trot on her own. I let her do whatever she wanted. If something disturbed her or caught her interest, she'd come back to a walk or would halt entirely to be able to look at whatever it was. After about a half a mile of traveling at a very fast trot, she picked up the canter of her own accord. I let her go. Then something strange happened. Instead of halting or slowing down to take a look at things, she'd just turn her head in that direction, and because she was always seeing things to the right and left that interested her, she moved under me like a snake (figure 169). Had I been an inexperienced rider, or had I been riding in an English saddle, this would have led to a parting of the ways more than once. A Western saddle gives you more security. As we moved around a corner we came upon a farmer unhitching two wagons from his tractor who let the hitch fall to the ground with a bang. Mini froze on the spot and felt as if she'd sunk eight inches into the ground. I dismounted and led her quietly past the farmer, which she a little nervously let me do. Then I mounted again and rode on. She didn't seem at all upset any more."

✢

It doesn't make any sense to punish a horse for shying at something that's frightened him. It's much better to try to reestablish his trust from the position in which he first learned to trust you—on the ground leading him. Of course for this to work the horse must have been well educated in hand in a less threatening environment.

*

"When I decided to start the ride home, Mini made it clear that she didn't care for that idea. She turned right around again and wanted to continue exploring. She's an unusually curious horse, hungry for information. Up till now, she'd never been able to satisfy these needs. So, on we went exploring the neighborhood. We came across another farmer mowing his field with a combine in full gear, a sight that would scare most horses. I was able to halt Mini and let her stand and look at what was going on. When we later came to other farm machines being operated, she simply went past them. I was always able to turn her around each time, however, to let her look. This was clearly due to the work in hand we'd done in the arena. In general, her newly won trust of people paid off under saddle."

On her excursions Mini worked only in the Lindell, a bitless bridle (see figure 155). Most Arabians work visibly better in one of these than with a snaffle.

*

Before we end this case study, I'd like to say a few words about riding Arabians. These born riding horses have gotten a reputation in the Western world for being unridable.

Mini moved under saddle with her head held up when she wasn't exploring something on the ground. Why did we allow this? Shouldn't we have made her carry her head lower and fixed?

Arabians were bred for the desert, where horizons are unlimited. For his rider's safety the Arabian needed to look into the distance, which was easiest with his head held high. If we force his head down so that he can't see, he's going to be nervous. This is what happens when we try to force our middle-European style of riding where it isn't appropriate. Lady Wentworth, one of the original importers of Arabian horses from North Africa to England, has said, "An Arabian that doesn't shy at everything that moves close by or in the near distance isn't a good Arabian. He should shy at the movement of a butterfly. He's been bred to carry his rider in safety day and night; to do this, his eyes must scan the horizon

**Fig. 170**

for the approach of danger."

The more purely bred a horse is, bred for a particular landscape and for a particular purpose, the stronger his inborn characteristics will be. An Arabian sees best with his neck carried at medium height and his head stretched forward, allowing his eyes full sweep of the horizon. Ridden in this fashion, Arabians are rarely hysterical.

\*

After only two weeks training, Mini's owner rode her through a grid of poles (figure 170). Mini knew her lessons well and confidently negotiated the poles on a long rein. Her head stretched low and alert, she picked her legs up high and moved with perfect balance. Her tail swung freely and quietly in rhythm with her walk. She was ridden in a Western saddle, not for her sake, as Mini didn't have a painful back, but to give her rider more security to be able to better sit out Mini's occasional shying.

Later Mini's owner wrote us: "I must admit that I didn't feel comfortable leaving Mini in Reken that first time. I wanted to believe that she wasn't going to be coerced, yelled at, or hit, but I'd really only known this kind of trainer. With much foreboding, I went to visit her on the following weekend. I wondered what would have happened to my poor, delicate little mare. I found her standing untied in the middle of the arena yawning and relaxed as she watched the other horses being worked around her! That hysterical little soul stood there quietly for fifty whole minutes—totally relaxed. Later she was led over cavalletti, across a plastic sheet, and through water! All this she did with quiet ease. After just one week, she was a totally different horse. The next weekend I was able to ride her on a hack with other horses. She was still nervy—she is, after all, hot-blooded—but when I got a little tense, I would say "Whooa," and she would halt and stand till my heart stopped beating quite so fast. We rode through a large and very noisy playground that I normally would have avoided riding through with the quietest old nag imaginable. I was the only one nervous, however. Mini just looked around with interest. Mini is back home with me now, living in a pasture with a shelter. She's well adjusted, friendly, and wonderful to ride. I've never again had the feeling that I wasn't going to come back from a ride in one piece. I did nearly fall off once. Mini had picked up a canter in the woods. Since we were headed toward home, I was a little ill at ease because I was used to horses who would bolt back to the barn if you let them. I think I must have said "Whoa!" rather emphatically, because Mini pulled the emergency brake, rammed her legs forward into the ground, and stood. This happened so abruptly that I almost went head first over her shoulder. Since then, I use the word only very quietly and that suffices completely. I think what impressed me most about my experiences at Reken, however, was Linda herself. If there is such a thing as the transmigration of souls, I'm sure she must have been a horse in a former life— probably one who was allowed to run free and wild across the prairies."

## DALI

One owner wrote: "My horse shies so badly that he's impossible to take on hacks. Once when I took him out against the advice of my friends at the riding club, he jumped off a railroad embankment onto an asphalt road. But he's like that in our indoor school as well. He jumps if he hears someone crinkling a candy wrapper. I always feel as though I'm sitting on a time bomb. He's also most difficult to tack and pulls his head up out of reach when I want to bridle him. I just don't know what to do."

We've chosen to introduce you to this last horse not really because of the nature of his problems, but more because of the cause of these problems. Dali was the nickname we gave to a giant of a horse with the grand name of Salvador. He was a seven-year-old Thoroughbred. Extremely well fed, he positively glowed. He was also very nervous and couldn't stand still for one second.

We asked his owner to ride him for us. As she was tacking him up the reason he fought being bridled became clear. The dropped noseband she was using was set too low and was buckled about three holes too tightly. Just as with thousands of other horses ridden in poorly adjusted dropped nosebands, this was painful to Dali. Yet this is how the owner had been taught to adjust the noseband at a rather renowned riding school. Every time he'd shy, she was told to "buckle it one hole tighter." (In figure 171 we'd already loosened it two holes. This had worried his

**Fig. 171**

owner, who thought Dali now would be totally unridable.) Here was the picture of a cramped, confined animal. The martingale was attached too short, and his rider rode him on a restrictive contact with the explana-tion that, "He needs to be ridden into the bit. Otherwise, I was told, I wouldn't be able to control him."

We aren't criticizing his owner. She'd bought an expensive horse, boarded him at a training barn with a good reputation, and was merely following the instructions of her riding teacher. What can we learn from his example?

Let's first look at figure 171. This horse is carrying his head stiffly and unnaturally high. This always happens when the rings of a running martingale are too low and pull the reins downward. The horse's reflex is to pull up. The stiffness this creates in the area of the head and neck then also restricts the movement of the horse's hindquarters. He can't bring his hind legs under his body and they trial along in short, choppy steps. His back is tight and he drops it away from the rider's weight. All this produces a jigging, unbalanced gait that is very difficult and uncomfortable to sit. This tense back, made even worse by the constant pulling, is often accepted as "getting the horse on the bit." But you can't get a horse to go on the bit this way—if the horse is really to be positively influenced by the rider's hand, he needs to be moving forward freely into the rider's hand from behind.

The pull of the rider's hand combined with the downward pull of the martingale not only conspire to stiffen the horse's neck and body, but cause him to hold his head so rigidly that he's incapable of looking around at his environment. When something frightened him, instead of being able to turn his head to see what it was, this horse could only roll his eyes in fear. When a nervous horse can't see he'll want to flee. The nervous swish of Dali's tail betrays his frustration and resistance.

We immediately got rid of Dali's martingale and raised his dropped noseband to act like an English cavesson. We left enough room between the cavesson and Dali's nose for two fingers to fit. Now it couldn't squeeze in on his nostrils or hurt the groove of his chin.

Fig. 172

We put a young student in the saddle and had her ride him, posting the trot to protect his tight back. She held her hands relaxed on either side of his withers, and maintained just enough contact that she could bring any sudden shy under control merely by bringing her hands back a little (figure 172).

It was as we had expected—Dali didn't shy. Compare these photographs taken within minutes of one another. In figure 172 Dali is relaxed. His hind feet are stepping well under the weight of the rider (the first prerequisite to riding a horse onto the bit). His neck is stretched and supple. His ears are forward and his eyes sweep the area taking in the environment. His rhythmically swinging tail now indicates contentment.

When we then started making threatening noises—even banging a chain against one of the barrels, Dali actually proved to be quite a quiet horse with good nerves. The noises didn't even startle him. He just turned his head to look at where the noise was coming from.

Dali was focused and alert during the T.E.A.M. exercises (figure 173). He negotiated the tight turns with no troubles. His handler kept Dali's attention with the wand and guided him through using body language (figure 174). She would take a step and he would take a step; Dali mirrored her movements exactly and was alert to her every signal.

During Dali's stay with us we turned him out in our paddocks and fields when he wasn't working. He enjoyed a happy fourteen-day

**Fig. 173**

Fig. 174

Fig. 175

**Fig. 176**

vacation. Able to move freely, he mingled with all the other horses and got himself into all the herd skirmishes.

After Dali had gotten through all the T.E.A.M. work in hand and had been ridden on hacks with no difficulty, we tested him by riding him with a simple neck wire, a test he passed with flying colors (figure 175). Elastic and alert, he moved without bridle or bit—and, of course, also without shying.

The change in Dali was so obvious (figure 176) that his owners decided to find him a place to live where he could be out with other horses as much as possible. Today he lives in a horse's paradise with another pasture buddy and his owner, whose whole family literally has moved to greener pastures.

We hope you enjoyed reading this book and learning about T.E.A.M. If you would like to find out more about T.E.A.M. you can write to:

T.E.A.M. Club
Box 5, Site 9, R.R. 8
Edmonton, Alberta T5L 4H8
Canada

You can also write to this address to receive information on ordering videotapes, T.E.A.M. equipment and products, and *T.E.A.M. News International*, the T.E.A.M. newsletter. *T.E.A.M. News International* publishes case histories and other T.E.A.M. news, lists clinic dates and contacts, and alerts readers to newly released T.E.A.M. articles, books, and videotapes. We are also very interested in hearing about your own case histories using T.E.A.M. and welcome your letters describing any experiences you may have had with any animal (pictures are wonderful too).

Please enclose $2 for shipping and handling.

# Index